ALAN SEARS
ON LIFE, FAITH, AND LEADERSHIP

TEPEYAC LEADERSHIP SERIES

ALAN SEARS
ON LIFE, FAITH, AND LEADERSHIP

TEPEYAC LEADERSHIP SERIES

PUBLISHING
Phoenix, AZ

About the Tepeyac Leadership Series

Tepeyac Leadership, Inc. (TLI) is a nonprofit organization dedicated to civic leadership development for lay Catholic professionals worldwide. The Tepeyac Leadership Series aims to provide inspiration and insights for Catholics based on contemporary models of lay Catholic leadership. TLI offers a catalyst development experience that equips lay Catholics to become virtuous leaders, influence the culture and serve the common good. Learn more at TLIprogram.org.

The editor, Laurie Strom is a Deacon's wife, grandmother, and a former Executive VP & COO of SAE Industry Technologies Consortia and Honeywell Aerospace Director, where she managed engineering teams in multiple countries. Now, she is a mentor, coach, writer, and photographer - praising God and finding science and faith beautifully intertwined. There is beauty in a job well done.

Assistant Editor, Julie Bernhard, is a graduate of TLI 2025 Cohort. She currently works as a marketing executive, where she leads marketing strategy and execution for a corporate real estate firm. In her spare time, she enjoys cooking, shopping, and spending time with her family.

Cover Design: Maria Fernanda Hernandez

Copyright © 2025 by TLI Publishing
www.TLIprogram.org
Phoenix

Scripture verses contained herein are from the New American Bible Revised Edition, United States Conference of Catholic Bishops (https://bible.usccb.org/bible)

ISBN: 979-8-9907711-2-3

Printed in the United States of America

Dedication

This book is dedicated to the first eight cohorts of the TLI program -
2018 through 2025. May they continue to deepen their faith,
prosper in their professional pursuits, and become the virtuous
leaders they are meant to be.

"O Mother, strengthen the faith of our brothers and sisters in the
laity, so that in every field of social, professional, cultural and
political life, they may act in accordance with the truth and the law
brought by your son to mankind." (St. John Paul II 1979)

Hail Mary
St. Juan Diego, Pray for us.

TABLE OF CONTENTS

(para. x) indicates the applicable paragraph number.

TABLE OF CONTENTS (CONT.)

(para. x) indicates the applicable paragraph number.

TABLE OF CONTENTS (CONT.)

(para. x) indicates the applicable paragraph number.

FOREWORD

A Lawyer Who Makes a Difference

I first "met" Alan Sears on paper long before I would meet him in person. He was impressive even then.

As a newly minted attorney just starting the practice of law, I was given a subscription to a magazine for young lawyers. I will never forget the cover of the Fall 1986 edition: four pictures of young attorneys on the front cover (one of them I would come to find out was Alan) with the accompanying subtitle "20 Young Lawyers Whose Work Makes a Difference." Each of the twenty lawyers was profiled with an article, in Q & A format, that set forth the nature of their work and some of the motivations that drove them to do what they did.

The magazine was, in effect, touting these young lawyers as up and coming stars in the legal profession. My recollection, almost forty years after the fact, was that, while all the featured lawyers were impressively credentialed, many of the causes they were advocating were decidedly secular.

Then I turned the page to the article about Alan Sears, whom I had, of course, never heard of before. I read the article with fascination. Alan was the Executive Director of Attorney General Edwin Meese III's Commission on Pornography under President Ronald Reagan's administration, exposing the evil and insidious effects of pornography on the souls (and soul) of the nation - an obviously countercultural and unpopular position in the elite halls of power.

I finished the article and concluded that he must be a committed Christian, boldly using his legal and other talents to build up the Kingdom of God. As I dropped the magazine on a side table, I remember clearly thinking, "Well, I will never meet him, but God bless him and his future work with great success!" Two years later, in the Lord's providence, he was my brother-in-law.

Alan Sears is one of the top Catholic leaders in the legal profession. And, like all true Catholic leaders, Alan is fearless, faithful and focused on the mission at hand.

Whether it was his service forty years ago exposing the evils of pornography, later building from scratch what became the world's largest - and arguably most effective - Christian religious liberty legal and advocacy organization (Alliance Defending Freedom), or now helping other Christian organizations better fulfill their missions (Kingdom Alliance Builders), Alan has tirelessly, humbly, and with magnificent fortitude never deviated from serving the Lord Jesus, His Church, and the broader society. Moreover, like all great Christian leaders, Alan has been utterly dependent on the grace of Jesus and always had the wisdom and the humility to realize that apart from Christ he could achieve "no good thing."

Finally, Alan, like all good leaders, is selfless - hiring the best people he could find, allowing them to shine, and never worrying about who received the credit for success. Unlike some others, Alan has always made Christ the center of his mission, eschewing and resisting the real temptation to make himself the center of the work and to think the success of the mission was all about him. Alan embodies the Lord's admonition that in the kingdom, the leader shall be the servant of all, and the first shall be last.

With his natural talent, Alan Sears could have built up a nice little kingdom for himself. The world is a better place because Alan, the true servant leader that he is, dedicated his legal career, indeed his entire life, to building God's Kingdom instead.

May God bless Alan Sears and may God bless us through his life's work.

By Nikolas T. Nikas
President and General Counsel
Bioethics Defense Fund

INTRODUCTION

The starting point that I really have with everybody is ...
John 15:5, my life verse, "Without Christ, we can do nothing."
(para. 224)

The Tepeyac Leadership Series aims to provide inspiration and insights for Catholics based on contemporary models of lay Catholic leadership. The objective of the book series and its intended focus is to showcase exemplary lay Catholic leaders. This book features Alan Sears, an American lawyer and the founding CEO of the Alliance Defending Freedom.

In an engaging question-and-answer interview format between Alan and Laurie Strom, editor for TLI Publishing, Alan shares from his own life the surprises and challenges God had in store for him - going from a Baptist upbringing and early political engagement campaigning for Barry Goldwater to founding Alliance Defending Freedom and building it into a one-hundred million dollar plus religious liberty organization. Alan's story reveals how Constitutional Originalism and deep Christian faith guided his mission to "keep the door open for the Gospel." *Alan Sears: on life, faith, and leadership* seeks to capture the journey of a faithful advocate whose strategic legal mind and sacrificial service inspire future generations in the fight for religious freedom.

The book is structured to give the reader an insight into three concrete areas: the life, faith, and leadership of Alan Sears. With the aid of the table of contents, readers may jump into the area or questions they want to learn about first and explore the rest at their own pace. The text remains true to the conversation with Alan, but some of the questions have been modified to provide a smoother transition between topics. All proceeds from the sale of the book go to funding the mission of Tepeyac Leadership, Inc. (TLI).

Thank you for your interest in the life of Alan Sears, your support for TLI, and the time you will dedicate to reading this book. We hope you find in its pages much inspiration to nurture your own life, faith, and leadership.

Part 1
Life

The ones that live faith: people love to work for them, they love to serve them, people would do anything for them, they go above and beyond for them. It was so interesting for me to have that experience: to see and to understand that this sauce that I've grown up in, this Christian sauce, whatever you want to call it, was really a very special thing in the world. It really worked and it really made a difference. (para.41)

---

1. Laurie: *Alan, thank you for doing this interview today. I'm looking forward to learning more about you - your life, faith, and leadership.*

2. Alan: It's a great privilege and honor to be with you.

3. Laurie: *Let's start with your childhood history and your earliest memories. Where were you born, and how many people were in your family growing up?*

4. Alan: I was born in Chattanooga, Tennessee. My mother always laughs and says that was the place we were closest to at the time she went into labor, and she thought it best to deliver there.

5. We lived in a number of different places through the years due to my father's career. He was a schoolteacher, a school principal, and then he went to work for what would now be called FEMA, but at the time it was called Civil Defense. It was part of the Executive Office of the President. He was hired when Dwight Eisenhower was there. That again required some moves, but wherever we lived, Kentucky was what I always considered home. Both my parents were Kentuckians; the greatest bulk of my family, the ones that are surviving still and two of my children, are Kentuckians. We weren't like military people, but we moved enough so when people ask me

where I'm from, I just say Kentucky is our home base. Then, if you get to know people well enough, you go through the litany.

6. I was the oldest with three sisters to follow. There was a pretty good gap between me and my baby sister. I went away to college the year she started kindergarten. I have one sister who is a year and five days younger than I am. People used to ask us if we were twins, and we'd say, "No, we're a year and five days apart," as kind of the stock answer.

7. My parents were people of faith. They were evangelical Protestants. On my father's side, two grandfathers, on both sides [paternal and maternal], were Baptist preachers. Most of my family in Kentucky were, and still are, Baptists.

8. So, I came from a Baptist background. I had very good, very godly, very loving parents. I never had a moment in my life where I experienced the insecurity and discomfort that all too many people know these days. I'm very, very, very grateful to them.

9. My father just made it into his seventies. He has been gone for twenty-plus years. My mother is 98, and she's in an assisted living center right now and still "sharp as a whip."

10. They [my parents] formed me. They shaped me. They taught us great morals and great values, which were among my father's top interests because of his background.

11. He was the first person on either side of the family to go to college. My mother was the first person in her family to do the same thing. She graduated from high school at sixteen and from college at eighteen. You could do that in those days. So, their number one goal was for us to have a "better life," and to get all four of their children through college; they made a lot of sacrifices. We all worked pretty hard. By the time I was a college senior, I had three jobs all at once in addition to my college studies. They basically set the standard and the guidelines and helped us all they could sacrificially. They achieved their goal; they got all four of their children through college, and a couple of us through graduate school. I owe a great debt to them.

12. My father had the most interesting job with the civil defense. People who are reading this probably won't remember the era of the Cold War and the threat of nuclear war, where children were told in the event of a warning to get underneath their desks! Being of a curious spirit, I always wondered, "Okay, if this is a nuclear bomb that's going to take out the world, what difference is it going to be if I'm under my desk or sitting at my desk?" But, you know, you don't ask questions like that!

13. My dad trained people from across the globe; people literally flew to where he worked, and he traveled quite a bit too. He trained people how to teach their populations to survive nuclear attacks. One of the things was that you had to have food in these fallout shelters. So, he would from time to time bring home the latest experimental foods. And again, in my childish way, I thought, "I'd rather be dead than have to eat this stuff for the next five years while I live in an underground cave!"

14. It was a different era in many ways, but we were taught great values because my father explained things to us about totalitarianism, about what had happened in World War II (which he served at the end of), and about communism. He explained the systems of government in the different nations, and how the personnel leading those systems of government made all the difference in the quality of life and in the type of opportunities that the populace had. So, his lessons impacted me in everything I do now, as "personnel is policy."

15. Laurie: *I can see that! Are there other people who were also influential in your life?*

16. Alan: I would say that there are several people that, at different points and with different focuses, had a tremendous influence on my life. I've already talked about my parents, especially my father, but another one of those people who had an outsized influence on my life was Edwin Meese III. Ed was the Chief of Staff in Sacramento for President Reagan when he was still Governor Reagan. He helped Ronald Reagan become President, and then he was White House Counsel until he was appointed as the 75th Attorney General and head of the Department of Justice (DOJ).

17. I was honored and blessed to be able to work in the Department of Justice after President Reagan took office. I served under Reagan's first Attorney General, William Smith, in the United States Attorney's Office, where I became Chief of the Criminal Section and led a number of federal task forces. Eventually I moved to Washington, detailed to the Office of Legal Policy, and I served as Executive Director of Attorney General Edwin Meese III's Commission on Pornography, and in other roles.

18. Edwin Meese III is actually the subject of a brand-new book, *The Meese Revolution: The Making of a Constitutional Moment.* The authors of this book assert that Meese was the most influential Attorney General in the history of the nation. What Ed did is really amazing, and most people don't know it. When Ed came into office, he was very concerned about how the courts were rewriting the Constitution. Our belief is that the Constitution, when it was written, had a very specific meaning for each word, and that we're not free to reinterpret those words. If we want to change the Constitution, there's a way to do it. It's called amending. He challenged the courts in a speech. How many Attorneys General speeches do you recall ever being given? Zero?

19. Laurie: *I don't recall any.*

20. Alan: The average American would say, I've never heard of any. You know, half the people might say, I didn't even know we had an Attorney General! But he [Edwin Meese III] gave a speech, a challenge on this issue of the courts rewriting the meaning of the Constitution. He called the courts to return to something called Constitutional Originalism. This isn't original intent, where you kind of get in the Founding Fathers' minds. This is just read the words and look at a dictionary from 1789. What did the word mean? Now let's apply it - whether you're talking about the Internet, the railroad, or a horse and buggy. The word still means the same thing. You know - Interstate Commerce, free speech, freedom of religion, etc.

21. Well, two Supreme Court Justices were so troubled by his assertion that they responded. Then he went on and gave us the speech again down at the American Bar Association meeting, and it became front-page news. Fast forward forty years, and every law school in America either has classes on the topic or uses class time to

talk about this principle, either to fight against it (oppose it), or to support it.

22. Meese revolutionized the way that Reagan tried to pick judges, and every Republican President since has been using this standard of Constitutional Originalism. It's how we ended up with so many Catholic judges on the bench because the concept of natural law is, shall we say, a biblical Constitutional Originalism. We don't rewrite the Bible. We don't rewrite scripture. We apply the terms, maybe even three-thousand-year-old terms, to the affairs of the day without changing the meanings of the words.

23. So, anyway, with that big background on Ed, I was honored and privileged as a pretty young man to be in the proximity of and report directly to the Office of the Attorney General. I got to watch this gentleman in action.

24. Two of my life principles that I've applied when I did anything later, and particularly when I built ADF [Alliance Defending Freedom], I got from him. I labelled one of his lessons as "making stars of others." This is something Ronald Reagan always did. I don't know if they [Reagan and Meese] ever used those phrases. I took that phrase from watching their lives.

25. Ed Meese was the most humble man imaginable. He wasn't falsely humble; you know, we have false humility, and then we have real humility. He was truly humble. He showed that basically, you influence more people by lifting them up and promoting them than you ever will by promoting yourself. This is so contrary to the Washington, DC mentality. It was breathtaking. It caught my attention.

26. The other thing that people didn't know about Ed - he was in a weekly Bible study. Here's the Attorney General of the United States, formerly White House Counsel, and he's in a weekly Bible study. He's a Lutheran. He barely ever missed it, no matter what, unless he was traveling across the globe. He never rubbed his faith in anybody's face, but it was so apparent that he lived by his faith. That had a great influence, too.

27. After Ed Meese left the DOJ, he joined the board of one of the first nonprofits I formed, served faithfully and attended all the meetings. When ADF was launched, he came to the public kick-off and over the years he traveled (for NO fees!) to speak for us time and again. When we launched the Blackstone Fellowship, he became a faculty stalwart summer after summer as long as his health permitted. He was later joined by another former Attorney General Michael Mukasey.

28. Ed would be one of the most outsized people in terms of influencing my life - seeing a public servant who's made such an incredible impact that most people don't know about. Probably at least a third or half of all the federal judges in the country have become judges because of the philosophy that he espoused, and every Republican President has used it since as a standard for judicial selection.

29. Laurie: *When were you in Washington working with him?*

30. Alan: 1985 - 1986, I was in DC with him. Then, I went over to the Department of Interior with another godly Christian leader, Secretary Don Hodel. He is another great, humble gentleman who was leading one of the largest departments in the government with control over massive amounts of resources and land. His faith guided him in everything that he did. This was just such an amazing thing to watch these Cabinet officers serving the President, who all knew God was a central part of their life.

31. Laurie: *I look forward to returning to that discussion of faith and leadership in the later sections of the book. But now I am curious, how did you get there? How did you end up in Washington working with them?*

32. Alan: I guess it started in eighth grade. I went door to door for Barry Goldwater in 1964. If you did enough doors, you got a little lapel pin. Remember that Barry Goldwater symbol with the black horn-rimmed glasses? You got a little lapel pin with those. I've got two of them still somewhere.

33. Because of my father, I was always interested in public policy, public life, and politics. I thought it made a difference, what little bit

I understood. Barry Goldwater appealed to me, so then in high school, I continued working on another campaign as a volunteer. So I was very active and very interested in government.

34. I had a tremendous government teacher in high school who talked about how one person can influence your life. He gave me a slogan that I've used as recently as yesterday in a consultation with a ministry. It was, "Durable base plus potential equals victory." That was his view on how you win in politics, and it's how you win in the world of charity, nonprofit and religious work. "Durable base plus potential equals victory." When I got to college, I got very active with the College Republicans.

35. Laurie: *Was that the university in Kentucky?*

36. Alan: Yes, I became the College Republican State Treasurer - a big, big job, State Treasurer! I think the most money we ever had in our treasury was like four thousand dollars - big money! But I got involved in a number of things. I actually dropped out of college twice, always with the intent to go back. I didn't do it to quit, but I got an opportunity to work in the Office of the Governor of Kentucky. So I dropped out for a semester and spent nine months working for the Governor. When he left office, I returned to school. Then I dropped out again to work when he ran for the United States Senate. Unfortunately, he wasn't elected, and I continued on my track to go to law school. I worked between my senior year in college and my entry into law school for a United States Senator. Interestingly, one of the people who worked for the same U.S. Senator was Mitch McConnell who later became the majority leader in the U.S. Senate for a number of years.

37. So, I got a little bit of exposure to volunteering and got to know some of the political world. When you're a young kid and you can stay up all hours of the day and night, one thing every campaign needs, no matter what your job, is drivers. The candidate can't possibly drive himself and shouldn't. You know, you're driving all over the Commonwealth at all hours of the day and night. I remember I found myself in the car at midnight in remote rural areas of Kentucky with a sitting United States Senator who had been all over the world. He'd served every President from Eisenhower through Nixon. I heard amazing stories and learned a lot of things,

but I also saw these people's characters. That was one of the other great lessons in my life.

38. I saw politicians who were just disgusting, frankly. As I got to know them and watch them, they were conducting adulterous affairs. They were just jerks; I mean bad people.

39. And then I saw others who were model citizens. What was the difference in all of their lives? It was faith! In my era, there was not a single politician who did not claim faith. But there were a lot of people that I saw who did not live their faith.

40. Laurie: *How is it different?*

41. Alan: The ones that live faith: people love to work for them, they love to serve them, people would do anything for them, they go above and beyond for them. It was so interesting for me to have that experience: to see and to understand that this sauce that I've grown up in, this Christian sauce, whatever you want to call it, was really a very special thing in the world. It really worked and it really made a difference. It was pretty special.

42. So, I saw the Executive Branch through the Governor's office, and I saw the legislative branch with what I was doing with the U.S. Senator. I saw both possibilities and limitations, even at that young age, with what the executive branch could do and what the legislative branch could do. I really felt led to go to law school.

43. I'll have to say one of my frustrations with legal education was that there was a very limited amount of fellowship with people who shared the same kind of values that I had. I had a couple of extremely good professors, and then I had a couple of very problematic ones, I would say, who taught us a very different view of the Constitution and America's origins than I had come to understand. They talked about something called the living, breathing Constitution; the idea that the Constitution was porous and that its meaning could change over time. It could be adapted. I had no formation in this, but I knew this was not the approach that I thought we should take. I knew that when the words were written, the words had specific meanings, and they were to be applied as they had been written. I found out [when

working with Edwin Meese] that it was called Constitutional Originalism.

44. So, I had some struggles with both the content of what I was being taught and the lack of fellowship. During that time I actually began to form in my mind what later became known as the Blackstone Fellowship because, I said, "You know, we need an organization that creates lifetime relationships and creates an opportunity for fellowship so that young men and women can have an opportunity to develop friendships, carry them forward and also have formation in those areas that I struggled to understand or to deal with because of my own lack of education at the time."

45. Then, with all of that background, I ended up doing some volunteer work in the first Reagan campaign, when he lost to Gerald Ford. When he ran again in 1980, I did a little work there; my former Governor became his Campaign Director for the Commonwealth of Kentucky. When Reagan was elected President, I was blessed to join the Department of Justice.

46. I served in the Department of Justice, the Department of Interior, and then back in the Department of Justice during George H.W. Bush's tenure (under Attorney General Bill Barr whom my daughter served many years later in his second term as AG.) As I moved, going back to college, finishing law school (1977), going into law practice, and with the various experiences and opportunities - I looked across the three branches of government and I saw what the government could do, what the government should do, and what it should not do. Fast forward to when we launched ADF, I had quite an array of experiences.

47. Laurie: *For those who don't know anything about ADF, what is it? How does it actually work?*

48. Alan: Well, Alliance Defending Freedom, when we launched it, actually had a very simple mission statement: It was to "Keep the door open for the Gospel, the good news of Jesus Christ." We looked at doing this in three different ways: through strategy, training, and funding to further advocacy for and to protect religious freedom, sanctity of life, and the family. Now we can talk about each of those: strategy, the idea was that we·all need to work in an alliance toward common goals. When we launched, there were quite a number of Christian legal efforts, but they weren't coordinated. You'd have one lawyer, one organization working over here on one problem, then another lawyer and organization working a different way, and sometimes there was great disunity.

49. I always remember, I was in Missouri and actually had a secular judge challenge me; he said, "I have a case before me involving a divorce with the parents wanting to have different dispositions for the religious upbringing of the children in the post-divorce status." The judge continued and said, "I have various religious organizations filing briefs that are opposing each other." He was a secular judge, and I think he made a laughing reference to Solomon and cutting the baby. [1 Kings 3:16-28] But he said, "As a secular judge, how, if you Christians, you religious people can't agree, how am I supposed to decide what the proper disposition of this is?" That always impacted me.

50. So, one of the first things we worked on was defining the areas that we needed to focus on the most and then developing, for lack of a better term, a strategic battle plan to take to the courts and to look for the cases that would further that effort.

51. With regards to training, there was again no organized training for lawyers or law students that wanted to be involved in this area. For example, you might be a real estate lawyer, very superb in your area, but you get a call from one of your major clients, and he says "My daughter was told that she could not have her Bible or her rosary on her desk at school. I want you to get that fixed today." And you know, Lawyer Sally, or Lawyer Sam, who gets the call may not have the first idea in the world where to look. It's so far out of their area of practice. And so, we said, "Let's develop a training network to train lawyers, at least give them an overview, so they will know where to look in this area."

52. The law student program we've talked about, the Blackstone Legal Fellowship, was intended to get people at a much earlier stage, between their first and second year of law school, and give them this formation. Then, as they go through school, they will have a lifetime resource.

53. So strategy, training, and funding: As we built a volunteer lawyer network, even though people might do pro bono work at no cost (which is a real sacrifice, and I think a lot of people don't realize what it requires to do something pro bono), we said, "Well, we need to have funding available for the costs and expenses because even if she or he is serving for free, they might have thousands of dollars in travel expenses, deposition court reporter expenses, and many other things." So ADF has now awarded more than fifty million dollars and more than two thousand grants to people the world would call competitors, that we call allies, to fund that ability.

54. More than three thousand lawyers have gone through some form of training and over four thousand participated in some way with the Blackstone and the Arete Academy programs and more.

55. So, ADF is strategy, training, and funding to further advocacy.

56. Laurie: *What is legal advocacy and how does it work?*

57. Alan: Advocacy ranges and covers everything, from legislative testimony, explaining laws or problems with laws or laws that need to be enacted (and that's somewhat different from lobbying) to providing testimony and expertise on various things to various forums, city councils, county governments, school boards, and similar, and then ultimately you have litigation. Lawyers always like to say litigation is the last thing we like to do because that means that everything else was unsuccessful. So, when you file a lawsuit, it means that the other side is just unwilling to work out a resolution. But that's what people mostly think of when they think of advocacy. There are many, many steps to getting there. ADF has probably mediated or informally resolved far more cases through conversations, letters, and different efforts than through going to court. But then God has blessed ADF to have a tremendously successful record in court.

58. Laurie: *Interesting! But when did you squeeze in graduate studies at the Stanford University Graduate School of Business, Harvard Law School, Harvard Business School, Catholic University of America, and Pepperdine University?*

59. Alan: Well, actually the graduate studies were what I needed to lead beyond your basic lawyer track [University of Louisville Louis D. Brandeis School of Law]. I had a period of time in private practice and I had a period of time with different firms, but when I started Alliance Defending Freedom (ADF), it was originally called Alliance Defense Fund, I didn't have an MBA. "I've been in the legal arena," I thought, "and I need to know more about how to manage people and run things."

60. We started ADF with one person and $4,700 bucks. By the time I left, we were at $70 some million - over a 1.6 million percent growth by God's grace. And now, it's more than a $100 million a year annual budget and 400 plus team members.

61. I realized the potential pretty quickly and I thought, "If this thing grows the way I think it may grow, I need an MBA equivalent. Because I'm starting this by myself, I can't just hire talent. I need to know some things." So, I began to look at all the graduate schools; everyone I talked to said Stanford and Harvard have the best business schools. I called them up [Standford and Harvard] and I said, "Hey, I'm a new CEO and I'm trying to build something." They sent me their material. So, what I did for quite a number of years is I went to either Harvard or Stanford every summer for these executive classes. We laugh because later we figured out I could have had about three MBAs for the price I spent for all this executive education!

62. You know, I probably spent more for a week than it would cost to get an MBA at a state school but probably saw one hundred million dollars in development as a direct result of my week with some of those professors; one was the only professor at Harvard to ever have a building named for him while he was still teaching there.

63. It was out of necessity that I did what I did. At Harvard Law School, I took some graduate courses; one of the things we had a real interest in was looking at international law. America was under siege, and we had Supreme Court Justices who began to cite foreign court precedents to reinterpret the U.S. Constitution.

64. The Commonwealth of Massachusetts Supreme Judicial Court quoted one of the provinces of Canada Court of Appeals as a means to fabricate something called same sex "marriage." Now the province

in Canada did not exist at the time that John Adams wrote most of the Constitution of the Commonwealth of Massachusetts. They reinterpreted what John Adams had said with this court opinion from a province that didn't exist at that time in Canada. Can you imagine? This is just crazy thinking! They were also citing the courts of Jamaica and other places in various cases.

65. So, I started a project at ADF to repel the use of international law to define what our rights are as American citizens. I didn't know international law, so I called around and they said, "Well, there's this professor at Harvard University, who's the best international law professor in the world. He wrote the book. It's the textbook." So, I called Harvard and I said, "I want to go to the class." I enrolled, paid a lot of money, and I had international law with the teacher that everybody said was the best in the world. I actually took two or three classes there that summer.

66. Laurie: *So, you're starting this organization and you're taking classes, but where in this sequence of events did the family fit in? How did you make that all work? What did that look like?*

67. Alan: Okay, I'll give you a little funny tale. We have a thing in our family called "Our Summers in the Hamptons." [But first, the background.]

68. I met Paula when I moved to Arizona after I left the Reagan administration. She's a native of Arizona. She was born and grew up in Paradise Valley. Isn't that a great name for a city?

69. Her father was involved with the law firm of Denison Kitchel, who was general campaign manager for Barry Goldwater. One of her not too far away neighbors was Barry Goldwater, and when she was at Kiva Elementary School, Barry Goldwater used to come over and talk to their classes. So, here's the boy who went door to door to work for Barry Goldwater in eighth grade, and now I meet this girl whose family is somewhat involved, at least by geographic and occupational things, with Barry Goldwater. Kind of a little funny beginning to the story!

70. Paula and I had children and the family grew. When we were called on to launch ADF, I realized very quickly if we were going to

raise the serious money to stay in business, I would have to become the chief fundraiser. You know the dream was I'd be this lawyer doing all these fun cases and winning all these religious freedom fights. But the reality is, without Christ you can do nothing, and without cash, you can do less.

71. So, I came up with the idea that the first summer we'd go out on the road and take the family. At that point I think we just had three young travelers, but it's hard to remember; I don't have my calendar. I can tell you we had at least one in diapers. And we said, "Okay, we're going to go out, and we're going to go city to city to meet with people that we have some kind of connection with and explain what we're trying to do." Well, we did that for fourteen years in a row.

72. Laurie: *Wow!*

73. Alan: Literally, the Monday after school was out, we would leave town. We would return about the Friday before school started again. Somewhere along the way we would find the Walmart, or Target, or whatever, and buy the school supplies that were on the school list. In the early days, the cellphones were pretty lousy and there was no Internet as we know it now. We got the AAA guidebooks and the AAA TripTiks that we would use to plan a route. So, you know, one summer we did the Pacific Northwest - very intense. Another summer we'd do, maybe the Southwest, another summer, the northeast. We would try to do three to four events a day.

74. At the very beginning, it was like: I'd be in San Antonio, Texas, and I'd have breakfast with a business executive, lunch with a doctor, and maybe dinner with two families and I'd ask them, "Okay, when I come back at the end of the summer, could you have a lunch for me with five other doctors?" or whatever. Well, we built it from that. So, by the fourteenth summer, we were doing three events a day, and we would have three or four hundred people at many of those.

75. Laurie: *What do you mean by event?*

76. Alan: Lunches, dinners, breakfast

77. Laurie: *So, when you just started out, was it just you speaking?*

78. Alan: It would be one on one. I'd be sitting at a table with somebody like you, Laurie, somebody in the aerospace industry, or a doctor or an entrepreneur. I'd say, "Let me tell you about this dream we've got," because I didn't have any results to show at the very beginning. That was the foundational basis to build the organization.

79. By the fourteenth summer, the way the schedule worked six days a week was: In the morning I'd get up. Paula would take the children to breakfast, and I would go have breakfast with ministry friends, which could be one (or by the end) to maybe a hundred people. I would give my presentation/ talk/ whatever and I would come back, load up the car and go to the next city to do a lunch event. And then we would load up the family and go somewhere next for dinner.

80. Sometimes we'd cram in four events. We might do a midafternoon or a dessert event after the dinner. But as those dinner events grew, I'd have to stay through to the end. Then we would drive after dinner to the next city to be in position for the next morning.

81. Laurie: *Amazing! So the children went to all these different parts of the United States?*

82. Alan: They saw it all and as things grew, we began to do international. I had frequent flier miles. I flew eight million miles on American Airlines, which is more than any Pope has ever flown, and I had scads of miles. So, I took my family with me when I traveled internationally for the longer trips, not for the short ones. And so, the children went to the conferences and some of the things we did in Europe. They had some pretty neat experiences.

83. So, this "Summer the Hamptons" thing, that's how we grew the organization [ADF]. We call it "Summers in the Hamptons" because after we got past the TripTik days, they started building Hampton Inns. Well, Hampton Inns did something unique. One of their defining differences (but now one that everybody does), is they had a free breakfast. When you're traveling on a ministry budget, free breakfast with children is a big deal. And, you don't have to go to a restaurant and order, so my wife could have more control on those mornings. So, we began to call our voyages "The Summers in the

Hamptons." Doesn't that sound a lot better than going door to door begging for money or saying "My summer as a Mendicant?"

84. And so that was "The Summers in the Hamptons." But even today, the development folks at ADF still meet with and see people that I met during those fourteen summers.

85. Laurie: *Nice!*

86. Alan: So, we stuck graduate school in the middle of those summers. And then later, as we began to develop, and eventually had the five offices in Europe, there was a lot of work we had to cover. So, as I say, I hauled my children to Rome. They all got to see some of the popes. We were very blessed.

87. Laurie: *So let me ask a question this way: What would you consider some of the challenges that you've overcome? That's a question that touches on a lot of different areas - your health, your family, your profession.*

88. Alan: Where do you want to start? With the Alliance Defending Freedom the first challenge was, I had this unbelievable assignment, this opportunity, and no money. This is actually funny now in retrospect.

89. There were thirty-five different apostolate and ministry leaders that had come together at various meetings and they talked about the need for a different type of approach to religious liberty law because essentially, we were losing; we were getting our brains beat out. Actually, even worse than losing, was that most of the cases were not even being fought. Just for example, you would have a State Attorney General or a county or city attorney assigned to defend a case challenging something filed by the ACLU, and none of those lawyers had any background in these areas of Constitutional Law. All of a sudden, they're dealing with something that's very unique and very specialized. It would be like going to a real estate lawyer and asking him or her to explain Canon Law section fifty-two, or whatever. It just doesn't work. And so many, many of the cases were being, as I say, lost by not being fought well or lost by default.

90. These ministry leaders said, "We want to do it." Well, there was a commitment for $250,000 startup cash. When I arrived, after I had quit my job, I had $4,700 left over after some expenses were paid to launch this thing instead of a quarter of a million. That's a challenge.

91. Laurie: *Yes, it is!*

92. Alan: By the grace of God, I had a new friend who later gave ADF $35,000 that tied us over to at least get paid for a little while. So, I had to make a huge decision in life. Do I be the lawyer that goes out and files some cases and tries to do something? Or do we build a financial base? And who else can do it? Because there's one employee - one team member. The other option was to quit and go back with my tail between my legs and ask for my job back. After prayerful thought, we decided to go for it. That's what led to this complete lifestyle change. Every dinner prayer for our whole family included this phrase - you're going to laugh - "God, we ask you to bless the ADF Team and our income stream." [Laurie laughs]

93. So, everyone said it; the children grew up with it. If you saw any of them today you could say, "Do you still pray for the ADF Team and the income stream?" Over on my wall [Alan points] is the ADF Daily Prayer. We formalized it. The whole team doesn't ask now for the income stream, but they ask for the income to be increased tenfold. But so it was in those early days. Tell me a nonprofit that has not had a financial crisis.

94. We had some incredible challenges. One of my favorite stories I like to tell is about when I knew that God was really going to stay in this thing - because you always wonder, you know! Paraphrasing Abraham Lincoln, "I don't want to ask God to join me. I want to join him." But [back to the story], it was Thursday, and I was using a payroll service. (The staff felt huge. I think we were up to three or four, maybe five team members at this point.) We had no money in the bank to pay the payroll. At midnight the payroll service would withdraw the money. I don't know if you have ever worked with a payroll service. They withdraw the money at midnight and issue the checks on Friday with direct deposit.

95. It's Thursday afternoon. I knew where we were financially, and I was getting increasingly worried - panicked! I was calling and

calling and I couldn't get anybody on the phone. The two or three people I got on the phone said, "No, we're not interested in it. God bless you! Call again." So, I'm sitting in my office pretty discouraged. Everybody's gone home. There's a knock on the door, because the door is locked, and I go to the door. It's one of the delivery drivers. And he said, "I was in the building earlier today and I failed to give you this package." It was an envelope. [Alan gestures the size of the envelope and the motion of handing it over.] I thanked him, and I tore it open. In it was a check for five dollars more than the gross amount of the payroll! The check was from someone I did not know. No return address. It was a corporate name, an LLC…something. To this day, we've never tracked down who that was from.

96. There used to be a thing called bank night deposits. I don't know if they even have those now, but I immediately walked over to the bank and put this in the night deposit. Then I called the payroll service; fortunately they had people there at the late hours and I told them, "I just put money in the night deposit and it will be credited in the morning." I guess they trusted me; the checks were issued. No team member was without pay. We never missed a payroll after that.

97. Laurie: *We call that a God Wink!*

98. Alan: Yes, so that was when I felt like, "Okay, God, you've shown me that you're going to take care of this." So that was a huge challenge.

99. The secondary type of challenge was attacks. The challenge of attacks was not by the mean people on the outside. We've had incredible threats through the years from people who demand tolerance. The people who want tolerance the most seem to threaten and want you to have the least freedom. But those are expected. Those are people who don't know our Lord, and who don't understand our faith. So, those don't really hurt.

100. The challenge is when people from within the faith community unfairly, and usually without full information attack, and they do it pretty brutally. We have had a couple of really, really serious challenges. In one case, after many, many attempts to try to mediate and to get these people in the room to talk about the facts and the truth, I had to hire a major law firm in Washington, DC; one of the

top slander and liable lawyers in the United States for a pretty good penny to bring this to a halt. Actually, when that law firm's letterhead appeared, one letter stopped the whole thing. I paid more for that one letter than some people get paid in a year. It hurt me deeply to waste those dollars and that people who claim to share our faith would falsely attack an organization on a completely meritless thing.

101. I had a couple of other instances with people that weren't that extreme, but it just always amazed me how people who claim to be part of the body of Christ would attack. We had this little saying, "Some people are so certain that they are right that they will punish you if you disagree with them."

102. One of the persons said, "We want to tell you how to run your organization." We told them, "We don't really want you to tell us how to run the organization." They started several months of attacking us. This is early Internet days, so it was mostly them writing letters to the editor. They got the IRS to do an audit, which was very expensive and very time-consuming. But it actually turned out to be a blessing, because the auditor was so impressed with the detail and the record-keeping we had, that they actually wrote a letter. We then sent our supporters the auditor's letter and said, "This is the result of the audit which some of you may have heard about with this publicity." Not only did we come out clean, we came out better than clean.

103. Actually, it got so weird. This person attacking us said we had bought a fleet of Cadillac Escalades. There was no basis for this whatsoever. I can't remember the number, but I think he said we bought a fleet of seven. It was preposterous, we had zero. But, you know, when there's no rebuttal, and in those days it wasn't the Internet where you could go up the next morning and correct the record, put your 990 [nonprofit tax form] up, or whatever. The reply for a monthly magazine was two months because the next edition would already be in bed before you could get the reply letter out. So, there were those challenges.

104. You also asked about health. I actually stepped down from ADF because of health issues. There's a long, long story here, but to quickly summarize, I got sick and had problems where I could not

perform at the level I needed perform, so I gave my board quite a long notice. The doctors couldn't diagnose me for a long time. My twenty plus year doctor saved my life because she finally found some people that could get the proper diagnosis, and by then, they told me I had limited time.

105. Well, one of my favorite little things that happened is one friend started a series of Masses for me at different places across the world. One of the Masses they celebrated for me was at St. Paul, Outside the Walls [Rome], which is one of my favorite churches ever! And I said, "Okay, so I have to get a death sentence to get a Mass at St. Paul, Outside the Wall!" I guess it's better than not having one!

106. But it was prayer, I am absolutely confident, and my doctors, and the surgeon. I've had eleven different surgical procedures with this thing, a course of chemotherapy, and a course of radiation, some of which are more brutal than the [stage four] cancer, I think. But here I am - past the time I was allotted.

107. Laurie: *Congratulations!*

108. Alan: That was a monstrous challenge.

109. Laurie: *We've talked about some of the challenges in your personal and professional life, but where have you found the most joy?*

110. Alan: Well, the greatest thing is obviously the family. I am blessed to have an incredible family. The size of our family is amazing to people. My wife's family has twenty-four cousins and on my side there are five. You add all this up, and then all of these people are getting married and having children. I don't think anybody can keep track of how many grandchildren, great grandchildren, and so forth there are now.

111. When we have these family gatherings, we have to do them at public locations with lots of room. You have everybody from the Diaper Squad, you know, crawling and squalling, to the people that are coming in in their wheelchairs and their walkers. So, I would say the greatest joy in our entire life, everything, every way, is family.

112. And then, my family members have all sort of reached out and "adopted" people, not in the sense of formal adoption. We do have some formal adoptions in the family, but we also have people that were "adopted" and invited to live with folks or have lived with them in the past. So, when we have these family gatherings, you almost need a roster.

113. I'll never forget a couple of Christmases ago, we were at one of these places and we were having our family Christmas madhouse - and it is a madhouse, you know. I asked my father-in-law, I said, "Who are all these little children? Do you know who they are?" He said, "I have no idea. Are they even related to me?" He was only half joking.

114. Laurie: *That sounds like a beautiful and fun family! St. John Paul II is often quoted as saying, "As the family goes, so goes the nation." You also mentioned the importance of prayer and faith. So, in the next section we are going to shift gears a little bit and talk about that faith!*

Life

St. Juan Diego Leadership for the World Award

Leadership

Alan and Paula with Bishop Thomas J. Olmsted
Induction to the Order of St. Gregory the Great

Alan and Paula with Pope Francis

Faith

Part 2
Faith

*I believe prayer does change things. It certainly changes the
approach that you have with the way you seek to bring about
change. I know that it certainly brought about a change in me.
(para.170)*

---

115. Laurie: *Alan, in the description of your life, you mentioned the
role models you had who were good examples of living their faith,
including Baptist and Lutheran. How did you go from a Baptist
background to Catholic?*

116. Alan: Like many, many people, I made, let's call it, a faith
decision. When I was in high school, I was convinced that Jesus was
the most important thing in the world. To use Protestant or
Evangelical terms that I had grown up in, I was born again. Actually,
it's a biblical term. Christ talked about being born again.

117. Then, when I got into college, like for a lot of people, there were
challenges to my faith. But I always knew it was true. I always knew
it was real and never had doubts. I just got a little bit away from it.
Then when I got to law school, I had a really serious challenge to my
worldviews because I was very naive. I thought I was going to learn
how to be a lawyer. I had this elusive idea that I wanted to get
involved in public policy. I didn't know if it was politics but certainly
in things that were somewhat related to what I had done
[volunteering for campaigns].

118. When I went to law school, I had a few very delightful
professors, who were the exceptions, but for the most part, it was a
very dark experience. I had a lot of professors who, like we talked
about earlier, believed that the greatest thing in the world was for the
courts to rewrite the Constitution. There was a term they used, "The
living, breathing constitution." There was also an incredible
arrogance. Obviously, there are exceptions to everything, but one of

the things that I noticed in law school was the number of people who had what I would call hard left or Socialist philosophies. Many were incredibly arrogant and demeaning to those who did not share their views. So I began to take some real abuse because I knew instinctively that much of what I was being taught was wrong.

119. In college, I studied a considerable amount of history. I was and I still am kind of a history buff. I ended up writing some history books myself. But what I learned in college is that a great deal of what was being taught in the classroom was not accurate history. I really began to understand how there are multiple sides to every story. Some of the professors - one professor in particular was enamored with the Soviet Union. He thought the only thing wrong with the Soviet Union was that it didn't encompass the United States, and I'm not joking! You know, he had a Hammer and Sickle on his Volvo. I mean a big Hammer. This is in the middle of the Cold War. We've got soldiers fighting and dying in Vietnam, and he's got a Hammer and Sickle on his car!

120. So, when I got to law school, I was thinking, I'm going to study contracts and torts, and things of that nature. But, when I got into the areas of philosophy, Constitutional Law, and so forth, it was just off the wall! And so, having had the history experience and education, I knew it was wrong, but I didn't know any basis to fight it. And I didn't have fellowship with too many people who shared my views. There were some veterans and some really nice people. You know how funny things are, there was actually one radically liberal woman who became one of my best friends because she discounted everything from the hard left. She thought these professors were so extreme that they were wrong. It taught me about the importance of alliances because this young woman and I found out we were not enemies; we agreed on more than we disagreed on, even though we would never vote for the same person.

121. I had an unpleasant experience in law school and because of it, I came up with the idea that if I ever got to a place in life where I could, I wanted to start some kind of a fellowship. That was a very important concept; a fellowship to provide a community of people who thought in a similar direction. I didn't have the word for it then, but I now know the word would be - formation. I knew that we wanted to have research and educate people on what we now call

Constitutional Originalism to counterbalance this flaky view of the living, breathing, rewrite it [the Constitution] every time philosophy. Their view is that when a judge puts on their black robe, they become like a god. They [the judge] can make the facts and the law fit the circumstances to come up with the outcome they wanted. I knew that was wrong. I knew there had to be standards. There has to be truth. There have to be certain things that don't change.

122. So, the whole law school experience was a challenge. Actually, a couple of classes I did the worst in were the classes that became most important in my life later because I had fought with the professors so much. Seriously, I was too stupid to know I didn't know anything, but I thought I did, and I could argue it till the cows came home. And so, God humbled me in a number of ways. I think, in Jeremiah [51:17], in one of the translations, it says something like, "All mankind is stupid and devoid of knowledge." That was like my theme verse at that flailing point in my life.

123. Laurie: *So now the theme verse is John 15:5. Right?*

124. Alan: Yes, "Without Christ, we can do nothing." But [pointing to his forehead and chuckling] I still believe "All mankind is stupid and devoid of knowledge." Christ gives us the ability to do something worthwhile.

125. From my bad law school experience, that's where the Blackstone Fellowship concept was launched, which now has nearly four thousand members. So, this again is how God uses things in your life that you think are bad for the good of His Kingdom. Because, I guess, if I had a really good, mellow law school experience, there would be no Blackstone Fellowship.

126. Laurie: *Is the Arete Academy similar to, or different from, the Blackstone Fellowship?*

127. Alan: Arete - that's a word from the New Testament that I think the Apostle Paul used [meaning best or highest form]. Arete Academy[1] is international now; when we originally launched it, we

---

[1] https://adfinternational.org/arete

had some Arete students in the United States. Basically, it is a shorter program than the Blackstone. But the idea is to develop leaders to take up positions of influence in law, government, public policy, media, academia, and other culture-shaping institutions. And most recently [2025], ADF added a new segment of ADF Arete for the British Commonwealth nations - those who have the commonality of speaking English. As some of our British friends remind us, we speak a form of English. They speak true English!

128. Laurie: *Yes, and they spell it differently, too.*

129. Alan: A lot of it, yes!

130. Laurie: *Let's return to the thread of becoming Catholic.*

131. Alan: Oh, this is another story!

132. While I was in law school, I was very, very active in my Baptist church. I felt a call to get into ministry. As I talked to my pastor, we discerned together that I should enroll in a seminary. I enrolled, and when I got to the seminary, it was worse than law school! Some professors said really unbelievable things. I had people who clearly questioned the divinity of Christ or the virgin birth! There was conflict after conflict, and it was not a good environment. It was darker than law school, which is hard to believe. I was getting a Master of Divinity in a dark environment.

133. There were some really fine young men in the school with me. There were ones like me who were just as befuddled by what we were being told in class. I found out the way you got good grades was to write on your essay tests, "In class, we have been taught this," and I would not give my opinions. I didn't phrase it quite that way, but I didn't say I agree with it. I just said, "This is what we've learned," because I didn't want to be a liar and say I agreed with it, but I didn't want to tell them what I thought, or they would zap me. Well, I finally reached the point where I couldn't do this anymore. I went to the Dean and told him I was going to drop out. We got into quite a little confrontation.

134. Well, this led me, along the way, to the Catholic Church Fathers. It took all that to get here. Along the way, in wanting to

disprove these professors, I thought, "Oh, I should go to the bookstore and the library, and I should go back and read the early Christian writers." You know what comes next?

135. Laurie: *Yes, but it never gets old! Continue!*

136. Alan: Well, I began to read the early Christian history to prove the Liberals wrong, and yes, there were some things wrong with the professors' teaching, and I began to read more.

137. Well, along the way, I get involved in the denominational fight. I've left the seminary. I'm out of law school, and I get elected twice to the governing body of this large Protestant denomination. I served on that for two terms. I was elected (twenty-five thousand people voted yes), and so I'm now one of the seventy-some members governing between conventions. I started out as a minority on the Conservative side. There was maybe a dozen of us. My second term ended when the Conservative group took the majority. I was term-limited out, but we saw a transition. Five seminaries got new Presidents. As a result of that transition, the seminary I was at, with a wonderful new leader, had something like a ninety percent faculty turnover within two years.

138. Laurie: *That is quite an impressive transition!*

139. Alan: So, there was hope, but I kept working and researching and reading. To do this, among other things, I eventually subscribed to a bi-monthly publication from *Our Sunday Visitor* called *The Pope Speaks*. It was about everything that Pope John Paul II said that was available in English. As I understand now, a priest named Thomas Olmsted [now Bishop Emeritus, Diocese of Phoenix] was doing some of the translation - from the Italian into English (which had been taken originally from Polish). It also had what we now call the Theology of the Body. So, I was reading all these things as they were being issued, within a couple of months after the pope's speeches.

140. Of course, with my political interests, I was watching what was happening: the whole thing with Karol Wojtyla [the future Pope John Paul II] standing up to the Communists, and then fast forward to my service when I went to Washington with Ronald Reagan. One of the ministry leaders who was involved with founding ADF was Dr. Bill

Bright, *Campus Crusade for Christ*. Dr. Bill Bright had been secretly sending money to Karol Wojtyla in Poland for his youth group. There's been an article written about that in *Christianity Today* that's probably available on the Internet. So, one of my evangelical friends had secretly been funding the ministry of the man who became Pope John Paul II! He wasn't his primary funding source, but this was obviously very dangerous with the Communists for the people who were carrying the cash. So just another little thing of how God works and people overlapping.

141. So, let's keep going with the story. I'm reading all this Catholic Church material. I'm in my second tenure with the Protestant governing body. I left the Reagan Administration at the end, and I'm out here in Arizona. I start dating this young lady that we've talked about [Paula], who is a cradle Catholic. Her father is concerned about her dating a Baptist. So, we get together, and we have two or three conversations at different times. He says to me, paraphrasing, "Why _____ aren't you a Catholic?" And I said, "Well, nobody has asked me." He said, "Well, why don't you look into it? I'm asking."

142. He introduced me to Father Ernie Larkin who was head of the Kino Institute; It was kind of the graduate school then in the diocese. Father Larkin and I did private instruction for several months. We used the Catholic Catechism by John Hardon because the new one wasn't out yet. Oh, and you'll love this - after we finished with our catechism session and our instruction, we then argued politics. I was a diehard Reagan supporter, and he was not, so we had good camaraderie arguing about this.

143. So fast forward, Paula and I were engaged and we went through, of course, the Church's instruction and all the prep. Father Ernie Larkin celebrated the Mass for our wedding.

144. Laurie: *What a fantastic journey!*

145. Alan: Yes, but like a lot of converts, I had some of my friends leave our friendship for a period of time. They were not happy with the choice I'd made. They thought I was pretty dumb, but eventually every one of those friends came back to be friends again. One of those who was the most condemnatory became very close to me again. Interestingly, a couple of those people are now in the Church themselves.

146. Laurie: *Funny how that happened!*

147. Alan: So, here's the moral of the story: If you're fervent in your faith outside the Church, don't read the Church fathers because you'll be disturbed, and you might end up in the Church.

148. Laurie: *I've heard that more than once!*

149. Alan: The swim across the Tiber is very precarious.

150. Laurie: *It's pretty amazing that you "swam the Tiber to become Catholic," and then you and Paula were several years later knighted by Pope Francis into the Order of St. Gregory the Great, the highest honor that the Pope can bestow upon laypeople. How did that come about?*

151. Alan: Well, I don't know! That's an interesting thing. I got a call; I literally was sitting where I'm sitting right now in front of the same computer screen that I'm talking to you on. I had a phone call from Bishop Olmsted; Bishop and I have, I think, a very cordial, very good relationship, so it was not usual for him to place the call himself. He said, "I'd like you to come downtown and have lunch." And I said, "Well, Your Excellency, I'd certainly be delighted to do so." (We'd had lunch downtown a few times before.) I said, "Could you tell me what it's about?" He said, "I'll just wait until you're here."

152. Then I don't remember all the details; I think they turned me over to his team to set up the time. They asked Paula to come as well. So, Paula and I went downtown. We literally, now you'll laugh, thought maybe we were in trouble! You know, because of all the activism that we have done, and our outspokenness on different issues. We were trying to go over in our minds, "Had we done something to make his Excellency upset with us?" And so, you know, we were searching…kind of like (you'll laugh) being called to the principal's office!

153. But it was so odd for us not to know the agenda, because normally, when you go downtown, you know - such as, we're going

to meet with a group of deacons and talk about something at the schools or Catholic education because I've been on the Diocesan School Board.

154. So, Paula and I go down to the Diocesan Pastoral Center, and we're sitting in the Bishop's outer office. His Excellency comes out and says, "Come on in." When we walk in, there's a small group of our friends and there's a cake! Bishop Olmsted proceeds to tell us that we've been appointed and that the Pope has selected us for this Order of St. Gregory the Great. He shows us a copy of the decree. (He didn't have the big certificate; the thing is huge!) He had a smaller copy of each of them [Paula's and mine], and my first question was, "What do we have to do?" His Excellency said "Nothing." Then he said, "This is one of the few honors you get in life where you're not expected to contribute or do anything. This is for what you have already done." Then he read the letter to us that accompanied it, and we both were moved to tears. We were pretty taken aback.

155. Laurie: *So, it was a complete and total shock!*

156. Alan: Out of the thin air! And then, of course, he had the ceremony to install us. I've got the invitation on my wall; somebody gave me a framed copy of the invitation for the investiture. We did it at St. Bernadette Catholic Church, and the Bishop presided. He came up with some antique vestments that were appropriate for the occasion.

157. As we understand it, there was only one other Knight and Dame recognized in Arizona history; that was the founder of Discount Tires and his wife. *The Catholic Sun* did an article on it a while back. So, it's Sir Alan and Lady Paula.

158. Laurie: *I will remember to refer to that going forward!*

159. Alan: We haven't used the titles too vigorously, but it was a great honor. And, of course, when we were doing the investiture, we made a commitment that we would serve faithfully for the balance of our lives. We take it very, very seriously.

160. Laurie: *Sir Alan, that is wonderful!*

161. Alan: Oh, I'll tell you another funny little story! We went to Rome; I've been there several times for different events, and we were going to meet with the Holy Father as a group. I was asked, "Where is your St. Gregory ribbon?" And I said, "Well, I've got it in my pocket." I think he said, "Put it on; the Holy Father needs to know you're one of his appointees." I can't remember exactly what was said. You know how in those moments you don't remember the details! Paula and I got our ribbons out and put them on and we had a few nice moments with Pope Francis.

162. Laurie: *What a great memory to have!*

163. *So, with Pope Francis passing away, do you have any thoughts or comments?* [Editor's note: interview was conducted on April 29, 2025, before the start of the Papal Conclave. Robert Francis Prevost was announced as Pope Leo XIV on May 8, 2025.]

164. Alan: I think I'm probably like almost every other person - we just pray that the Holy Spirit will be with the conclave. The world is so broken up, so divided, and there is so much challenge in the Church; we just ask the Holy Spirit to pour out and take control of hearts and minds. We want someone who wants to do God's will, whatever that may be in their lives.

165. So, a little side note on family faith: When we did those fourteen "Summers in the Hamptons," and also when I traveled an average of two hundred days a year for twenty-six years, wherever we were, we would go to Sunday Mass and some sometimes weekday Mass (but usually with the morning breakfast event you couldn't do a daily mass). But anyway, we saw every kind of parish in the world. We saw some of the most wonderful, gracious, great priests with beautiful celebrations that my family loved.

166. And then we saw the opposite. We saw some just horrible, horrible ones. There was only one Mass where I actually called my Spiritual Director and described what had happened. He said that it probably wasn't a valid mass because, among other things, they prayed the "our mother." You can't make this up. And it went downhill from there.

167. Laurie: *Oh, my! Speaking of doing what God wills in their life, what can laity do to help address the scandals in the Church - the lack of adherence to Church teachings, poor liturgy practice and outright abuses?*

168. Alan: Number one, in my view, is the formation of yourself. I mentioned I was very blessed when I came into the Church because I had Father Ernie Larkin for catechesis. Father Larkin was head of the Kino Institute, which is a very important training center in the diocese. I mentioned we used the catechism of John Hardon, and we spent a lot of time with that because the current catechism had not yet been released by Pope John Paul II. Then subsequently, when the new catechism came out, I bought the first edition. I got it about as quickly as you could get it and read it cover to cover. I also got [he looks toward a book on the shelf in his office] the Code of Canon Law and I read it cover to cover. I'm not going to tell you that I've mastered either one, but when I've had questions, I've gone to both of those books as well as others. Like I talked about with Blackstone, I've tried to form myself with the teachings of the Church.

169. Just recently I was involved in a men's Bible study made up of men of different denominational and faith backgrounds. I did a teaching on the seventeenth hundredth anniversary of the Nicene Creed. Some of these friends had never heard of the Council of Nicaea. They had never heard of the Nicene Creed before. So, we went back to the basics and talked about what happened through A.D. 325, about Apollinaris, Arius, and the heresy, and how important it was to establish the doctrine of the Trinity as we now know it. So I think that the first thing is to form yourself so that you're not talking with hot air and puffery. You're talking from a knowledge base.

170. Secondly, prayer: I know you can have four hundred hours of debate, but I believe prayer does change things. It certainly changes the approach that you have with the way you seek to bring about change. I know that it certainly brought about a change in me. I can use school board experiences as examples, both when I was on the local school board and the Diocesan School Board, and other positions. We've heard a lot of funny things and rather than lashing out or trying to condemn someone you think, "Lord, how would you want me to approach this person to hopefully help them see the error

of their ways, if, in fact, it's truly erroneous?" Sometimes we are quick to judge, and they may not be erroneous.

171. I'll just give you one little story about one of the assignments that was given on the School Board. Father (one of the priests) and I were assigned to help draft the first set of regulations for Catholic schools in the Diocese of Phoenix. One of the first items we put in the draft regulation was that every Catholic school in the diocese needed to proclaim in a very open way in its signage that it was a Catholic school. It got pushback! I won't tell you from whom or how, but people said that making this too obvious might hurt some of the enrollment in some of the schools because so many non-Catholics go to the schools. Even though they [non-Catholics] know it's a Catholic school, the non-Catholic parents might not be happy to have their children go to a school that was too Catholic looking!

172. Another regulation was that every classroom needed an image of the Virgin and a crucifix; that wasn't too controversial, but we even had a little pushback on that. One of the high schools had some parents who were of a different faith background and were very upset about the pro-life activities on campus, and the fact that on the anniversary of *Roe v. Wade*, during the March for Life, the school had prayer time, and teaching about the sanctity of life. We even had people in our own Church who were concerned about being too pro-life and maybe turning off these students and their parents who didn't share our views on the sanctity of life.

173. So I've seen a few instances of needing to work with people, and there are many, many others, but those are just a few that come to mind quickly. In each of those cases, I think we were able to address them and come out with the right response.

174. **Laurie:** *Perseverance.*

175. **Alan:** Perseverance. Yes, but again, you can't just slap them and say, "That's what the Church teaches." That doesn't usually win.

176. **Laurie:** *So where do you think there's the greatest need for the laity to serve right now?*

177. Alan: I think it's unlimited. I can't think of an area where there's not a need for the laity to be involved. I don't know of any bishop or any priest who has too much help. One of the things that I know is that many priests and many bishops don't know how to use lay help because they haven't had it. They don't know how to utilize meaningful volunteers, and sometimes they've had bad experiences with people. You know, like the Parish Council all of a sudden gets some renegade on there that thinks they're the mini pastor. Again, it's a formation issue, but I just think there are unlimited opportunities. I mean, think about every need that the Church has!

178. Talking about the service to the poor, Paula and I've been blessed to be part of supporting St. Vincent de Paul for twenty-plus years, maybe longer. I know that they have not run out of need for volunteers yet. They have not run out of a need for funding. You know, we all want to see the day that all those ministries and apostolates are closed down because there's no need. But in the meantime, there's everything along the way, even in areas of controversial issues.

179. I think all of us have sat in a Mass with a solid priest doing a homily on issues that are important to us, and we've seen people get up and walk out. You know, they make a kind of show of walking out. For some reason they always seem to sit there in the front, or they'll make a crack to Father at the back.

180.Think about how many times you can encourage a priest. Have you ever known a priest to say, "I don't want to be thanked again. I don't want to be appreciated." I haven't. So we try to make it a habit every time we hear a good sermon, a good homily, to thank the priest for delivering it and for his courage. For some of these things in this moment, it's courageous to just say the most basic things. In some forums, it's particularly difficult. So that's something important that the laity can do; there's not a single person who can't support a good priest.

181. Laurie: *Right! And I think of the St. Therese of Lisieux prayer for priests. That's one of my favorites and you have some favorite prayers too, right? What are your favorite prayers, and why are they your favorites?*

182. Alan: Well, which one do you want me to talk about? We could talk about just the simplest of all prayers, and that is the *Our Father*. That's one of my favorites. Also, "Jesus, I trust in you." Another one is just calling on the Lord to help us, "Come, Lord Jesus." You know, just asking him to be with you, or simply the Jesus prayer, "Jesus, Jesus, Jesus."

183. Laurie: *There's power in the name! You also mentioned a night prayer as one of your favorites.*

184. Alan: Yes, "Jesus Christ, my God, I adore you and thank you for all the graces you have given me this day. I offer you my sleep and all the moments of this night. I place all my loved ones, wherever they may be, in your sacred side and under the mantle of Our Blessed Mother. Let your holy angels stand watch and keep us in peace. Amen."

185. You'll love this - it's posted in the bathroom! So that is one we do nightly. We have a picture of St. Michael hanging next to it. Just a simple reminder of our need to pray and praise in the moment.

186. All of these prayers are favorites. And of course, St. Joan of Arc is one of my personal heroes, whom I admire so much. I don't know if you ever read the Mark Twain [Samuel Clemens] book, *Joan of Arc,* about her. The introduction is far better than the book, in my view, but he thought it was his greatest work. He was very disappointed by the commercial failure that it was. Here he [Mark Twain] was as an agnostic, and after he spent years studying the two transcripts: one from the original trial there in Rouen, France, and then the acquittal in Notre Dame in Paris. He became convinced that it had to be otherworldly. I don't know if he ever concluded it was God, but it had to be otherworldly: her vision of St. Michael and the other saints in her earliest childhood and, of course, her amazing, I think it was a prayer, at the burning stake. My favorite part of the story, which I believe to be absolutely true, is when the Dominican held up the crucifix, and she said, "Hold it higher, so I can see it above the flames." What an amazing thing!

187. One of the things we do know is that she didn't want to do what she did, but she was called to do it, and so she did it. As I said earlier, I don't think we're supposed to seek to be in positions of power. I

think we see where God leads us. I never sought to lead ADF. A group of people came to me to do it.

188. Laurie: *[Jokingly] You didn't do it for the awards? You have received so many! You didn't do it for the money?*

189. Alan: Well, in the beginning, I can tell you, it certainly wasn't for the money! Things were so tight at the beginning that we sold our house and moved in with the in-laws. We invested what we had in making the thing run. We used our personal credit as part of the deal. So, at the end of the line, the board was generous enough to give me some severance that helped me make up for the fact that I didn't have savings earlier. We're still very middle-class, I will assure you.

190. You know, St. Joan of Arc, at the end of the day, her reward was to be burned at the stake. She was betrayed. She was mistreated and then suffered this horrible death. And then, remember, they took her ashes and put them in the River Seine because they didn't want anybody to have a grave to go to. Nice people! I've been at the site in Rouen where she was burned at the stake, and sadly, the plaque is about the size of a computer screen. That's all there is. But she was acquitted on retrial at Notre Dame.

191. Laurie: *Yes, even then, retrial makes a difference!*

192. Alan: That was her mother, by the way; that's something a lay person did. Her mother drove the Pope nuts. I mean that probably isn't how the academics would say it, but she drove the Pope crazy until he had the retrial and then St. Joan of Arc was acquitted. It's a little hard to reverse the judgment.

193. Laurie: *Yes, wow, that is again perseverance!*

194. Alan: And by the way, across from Le Bûcher de Jeanne d'Arc in Rouen is La Couronne, one of the best restaurants in all of France. It's where Julia Child discovered the difference between cooking and Cuisine. It ultimately inspired her TV show.

195. Laurie: *I hope one day I can visit and be inspired by St. Joan of Arc's courage and have great French Cuisine too!*

SUGGESTED REFLECTION

St. Joan of Arc

She heard the flames crackling below her, and immediately distress for a fellow-creature who was in danger took possession of her. It was the friar Isambard. She had given him her cross and begged him to raise it toward her face and let her eyes rest in hope and consolation upon it till she was entered into the peace of God. She made him go out from the danger of the fire. Then she was satisfied, and said:

"Now keep it always in my sight until the end."

> — Joan of Arc by Mark Twain

"Lift high the cross so I may see it through the flames...."

> —St. Joan of Arc

> Remembering this great saint canonized 100 years ago today!

> National Catholic Register May 16, 2020[2]

Facing page: Paintings by Louis Maurice Boutet de Monvel[3]

The Vision and Inspiration (Joan of Arc series: I)
c. 1907-early 1909

(Saints Michael the Archangel, Catherine of Alexandria, and Margaret.)

The Maid in Armor on Horseback (Joan of Arc series: III)
c. 1908-late 1909

The Trial of Joan of Arc (Joan of Arc series: VI)

c. late 1909-early 1910

----

[2] https://www.facebook.com/NCRegister/posts/

[3]French Painter, 1850 -1913, Courtesy National Gallery of Art, Washington

Part 3
Leadership

Well, I think everybody's a leader. I think we lead in everything we do. Every aspect of our life is a gift of God - in our role as a daddy, as a husband, as a wife, as a mother. If you're a single person - in your circle of friends, in your work and in what you are assigned to. (para. 200)

---

196. Laurie: *Alan, you have already talked a lot about leadership because it's just part of who you are. It comes across clearly. Given everything that we've discussed about life and faith, why should one strive to be a leader? I mean, who can be a leader? And why? Why would they want to be a leader?*

197. Alan: I actually don't urge people to strive to be leaders. I urge people to do whatever God has put before them the best they can possibly do it and then suggest that they'll probably be selected to be a leader.

198. In my life, that's how everything in the world has happened to me. I got, you know, an assignment and no matter how cruddy it was, I tried to do my very best. The really funny thing about the many different positions that I have held in my life is that I've only applied for like one of those. Everything else was people seeing me and approaching me.

199. Laurie: *So how would you define a leader then?*

200. Alan: Well, I think everybody's a leader. I think we lead in everything we do. Every aspect of our life is a gift of God - in our role as a daddy, as a husband, as a wife, as a mother. If you're a single person - in your circle of friends, in your work and in what you are assigned to. Maybe this is where we're getting into definitional stuff, but I think we need to learn to lead what we do and to be like those people that I told you about who meant so much in my life. They showed me how their faith mattered, even when they weren't preaching to me and doing "God talk." They weren't going through the Catechism or through their Protestant belief system with me: They were just living it. They were doing it.

201. I don't know if St. Francis of Assisi actually said, "Sometimes use words." You know, how Winston Churchill is quoted as saying everything and anything, as is Abraham Lincoln, and St. Francis of Assisi apparently is quoted as saying everything too. So, I don't know what most historical figures really said, but we all have these stories of great leaders because of their actions.

202. I remember one of the jobs I had in college. I worked at a golf course. We did maintenance in bad weather, and in good weather we mowed grass and did outdoor maintenance of this golf course. I remember a couple of maintenance men who worked there who were very profound Christians. Nobody ever told me they were Christian. They didn't talk about their faith. After a while they opened up and so forth, but they just set an example. They'd always volunteer for the cruddiest jobs. One of the most difficult things in those days was when you aerated greens. You had to pick all these plugs of grass and dirt up with shovels. It was really horrible work, because you'd be doing it during a really humid time of year. You know, it's like ninety-five degrees and a hundred percent humidity. So, one man is pushing the wheelbarrow and another one is doing the shovel.

203. And these men, they would volunteer to do the worst part, the shovel part. They'd say to us, "So why don't you get the tractor and bring the wagon." Is that leadership, or what? Their example sort of shamed you into wanting to do it for the next person. So, even if you didn't really want to volunteer to do the cruddy job, you felt like you had to, because they set such a good example.

204. Laurie: *So, you talked a little bit about golf and lessons learned when you were young. Didn't you also do a stint as President of the Country Club at DC Ranch?*

205. Alan: I did. Yes. During the latter time at ADF, we started doing some golf events and golf tournaments because a lot of people of faith who have means like to have places other than restaurants to meet and talk. One of the places that you can have a good four-hour conversation is during a game of golf. So we started doing events, and I took golfing back up. I joined the club to have a good meeting place for friends of the organization - a safe place and a place where people enjoy being.

206. So, to make a long story short, like everything else I get involved in, I was elected to the board, then served as Vice President, and then became President for two terms. We did a lot of upgrades to the club, and we saw the membership value increase significantly.

207. Laurie: *So how do you find balance? You have served on a number of boards, Knights of Columbus, and many others, but how do you balance all of that with "earning a living?"*

208. Alan: Well, of course, when I was working the intense hours, I limited myself to two or three boards. I never served on more than two or three boards at a time, like being on the School Board of Catholic Education and maybe one other board while I was running ADF. But I just made it part of my normal calendar. One of the things I always did was get all the meeting dates scheduled out a year or two ahead of time. Then, as I began to wind down working for ADF, I got to the point where a year ago I was on nine boards, which no one should ever do; that was my self-inflicted pain! But I'm down to five boards now, and they vary in intensity. Some of them require a couple of hours a week. I've got one that, for a while, was requiring half my time! It was an organization that had many challenges and we had to spend a great deal of time working through it.

209. It can be a significant time commitment. I just got back; I was in Southern California two weeks ago from Sunday till Thursday on a strategic planning effort with one of the apostolates that I serve on. It was a great time of fellowship with a group of great people, and we came away with some really good understanding and agreement as to where we want to take the organization. Sometimes I have meetings that don't go so well. And then this immediate past week, I spent three days up in Sedona with the Alliance Defending Freedom team.

210. Laurie: *Why would you encourage a lay person to go on a board or serve on a board?*

211. Alan: First of all, serving on a board is a real way to grow yourself. When you're just in your work position and you're leading your life, you have one set of things that you're dealing with - one set of commonalities. When you get on a board, you really learn to see different views, different opinions, and different approaches. One of the things that is really fun on a board is working on common opportunities and problem-solving.

212. I don't like goal setting; I can't stand goals. I like to look at opportunities. We're all different in the way we approach it, but I think some of the most enjoyable moments I've had, even in the midst of some hard work, was developing some of the friendships I have on boards and developing the problem-solving skills.

213. I wish we had a simple board instruction guide. There are a lot of paperbacks out there you can order on Amazon and I've recommended a couple of them, but there's no really great one. They're good, but not great because of the diversity of boards. Every time I do any teaching for the Tepeyac Leadership Initiative, or for different groups, I always talk about why I think it's so important to be on the board.

214. Back to when you asked me, "What's the responsibility of the laity?" Again, if we leave all of the boards and so forth to secular people without values or without the values we share, is it any surprise that corporations and charitable organizations go off the rails? All of a sudden, you find a group that was founded to deal with juvenile health issues and birth defects is now advocating abortion. How would something like that happen if people of faith had been occupying the board?

215. So, there are multiple facets to it. You can really serve the board and serve the common good, the public, but you also can be incredibly rewarded for it. I will tell you one thing, if people want to go on a board to develop a resume and enhance their own reputation, they'll be very disappointed. Because, when your motives are improper and twisted, you won't put into it and you won't get out of it what you want. I've seen people do that and think, "Oh, I've been invited to serve on the X board, and that'll look good to my law

firm when I come up for partner." Huh? No. It usually doesn't if you don't care about the issue. You need heart alignment.

216. When I served on school boards, I was very interested in them because I had children involved. Even after my children were all out of secondary education and were no longer at the schools, I still had an interest, because, you know, thinking about grandchildren to come in the future, and that sort of thing. But if you don't have any interest in children and their future, why would you be on the school board?

217. Laurie: *Throughout the discussions on your life and faith, there is a clear thread of seeking the truth. You have done a lot to fight for the truth, incorporate it, and be a leader by passing it on and sharing it with others. You've done this both as a layperson in the Catholic Church and even more simply as a person of faith. What can you share with us about that leadership experience?*

218. Alan: What I did [starting Blackstone, Arete, etc.], I did because I saw the result of bad formation, whether it is Evangelical, Protestant, Catholic, whatever. But within the faith community, we saw the ill effects of so much poor formation; so much thinking that it's all about me, or, you know, "I'll fit the Scripture to whatever fits my philosophy." And then we saw the equal side of the poor formation of so many people in leadership, or the complete lack of formation, as we built the Alliance. ADF has now given more than two thousand grants, totaling more than fifty million dollars, to other organizations and lawyers, to those who the world would probably call our competitors. That was a real key part.

219. Back at the beginning, we assessed three things that were wrong with the pro bono legal movement: the lack of strategy, the lack of training and the lack of funding. We said, "We're going to try and provide strategy, training and funding." As we began to do this funding and began to start training in the legal areas, I began to see why so many of these groups and organizations were not doing well. And you hit the key: it was because the leaders were struggling so much.

220. One of the things I discovered is that a lot of these organizations weren't growing, not because the leader was a bad person or they

were bad, they just were clueless on leadership. They had no idea! And so, I began to take some graduate classes, and on my own, I developed a series of questions. I began to work informally, while I was still leading ADF, with some of these organizations. One of my basic questions was, "How do you define success? How do you define victory?" And you've never seen so many faces go blank so quickly when you ask the CEO, "How do you define success?" Now, you would think that would be the first thing that people would answer.

221. On one of my more recent calls, I was working with a young woman who had fairly recently been appointed to head a legal center; it's not a religious nonprofit, but it supports our faith values. It is organized as a secular group. She called me and she wanted to talk about fundraising. I said, "Well, I'll talk to you about fundraising, but first of all, tell me, how does your organization define winning?" She gave some kind of nebulous thing. I said, "No, what do you tell your prospective and your current donors what you are about?" She stumbled around, and I said, "Now, the most basic thing you need to know for fundraising is what you're trying to achieve."

222. So, what happened when I stepped down from ADF (and I thought, quite frankly, I was too sick to do anything and was told I was probably not going to be around much longer), I began to get all kinds of calls from people. They wanted three things. One group wanted me to be on their board, and I naively accepted too many of those. I ended up on, I think, the top number was nine apostolates. Don't do that. The second thing was that they wanted me to help with their fundraising, and the third thing was that they needed counseling on leadership. I sort of developed a specialty. I don't like to teach fundraising. I like to teach leadership, because if you do good leadership, fundraising can be a good byproduct. So, I finally narrowed it down [as Executive Director of Kingdom Alliance Builders] and I said, "I want to basically spend my time doing mentoring and consulting work with the health that I have, however long that is, with first-time CEOs."

223. I was thinking, "I'm going to be working with young people, which is always fun." And my! One of these first-time CEOs was seventy years old. There you go. A full life, everything they'd ever done, and then they are asked to lead an organization at age seventy;

that was kind of fun. The first thing I always say is, "No matter what you've done before, there is no CEO school because nobody has ever had the responsibility of your bi-weekly or monthly, or whatever it is, payroll besides you. Until you have that responsibility - it's on your shoulders and nobody else's - you don't know what being a CEO means."

224. I sent you forty years of life lessons that I tried to summarize. (See Appendix) But the starting point that I really have with everybody is even more basic: It's John 15:5, my life verse, "Without Christ, we can do nothing."

225. I have two criteria to accept a client to work with. I hate to say this on the record, but I will. Many people I work with don't pay anything. I have set fees, but when there are sob stories or such that they can't pay, oh, I always end up doing it, anyway. So, the two standards are: [1] Do you have a teachable spirit, and [2] Do you share our faith values? I have a little faith mission statement, which is basically the Apostles Creed. I always want to clarify because I've been led astray in the past, thinking somebody was well-formed, at least enough to mentor, but I found a couple of people who claimed to be a leader of a Catholic Apostolate, but didn't share the Church's view on a very important issue. I was stunned. That is a long side story. So, that's why I ask these questions.

226. The teachable spirit, though, comes out in about thirty minutes. I'm sure you know exactly what I'm talking about. For the ones that don't have a teachable spirit I say, "Why are you here? Why do you want help if you want to argue with me?" I don't do a second session with those.

227. Since I've been doing this, I've worked with almost one hundred different apostolates and CEOs. Sometimes I work with the boards and then work with the CEO. Sometimes I work just with the CEO, and occasionally I've worked with a CEO and some other C-suite person. But I always believe the CEO is the "chief cultural officer," no matter what they call themselves. As we all know, culture is everything.

228. So, after we get John 15:5 down, that you owe everything to and everything is dependent on Christ, then we can talk about vision and

values. "What's your vision? What are your values?" We want to teach that there are certain things that have to be non-negotiable. One of those non-negotiables is how you view your team. That's why I love the word team. It's probably an overused word now. In about fifteen or twenty minutes of discussion, you can find out what people think of their team by what they call them.

229. Laurie: *Yes, it is important to determine if they have the heart of a servant leader.*

230. Alan: Yes, you learn really quickly if there are different classes of team members. In the hospitality industry, I was honored to partner with the Ritz-Carlton, LLC., for over twenty years. The founder of Ritz-Carlton, Bill Johnson, said, "The cornerstone belief of the company," which they still have on the little card that every employee worldwide carries, is "We are Ladies and Gentlemen serving Ladies and Gentlemen."

231. This was a radical concept in the hospitality industry; that the ladies and gentlemen who worked on the properties had the same value as a human person as those who came in with the big fat wallet and could pay the bill. "We are Ladies and Gentlemen serving Ladies and Gentlemen," he literally changed the entire hospitality industry. A book was written about it called the *New Gold Standard* [by Joseph Michelli]. I brought in the Ritz-Carlton team to train my team on this concept of the "Gold Standard." This idea comes from "Imago Dei," [Image of God]; every person is equal in the eyes of God. We all have inherent value. I know that's one of Bishop Dolan's [Diocese of Phoenix] initiatives now with his new *Office of Human Dignity*. He has appointed a Vicar [Father Andres Arango, pastor of St. William Parish in Cashion, Arizona].

232. The "Gold Standard" works in every area. What was astounding in the nonprofit world was how badly a lot of organizations treated their team members. It was like, "How cheap can we buy the insurance? How cheap can we get them to work here because they're dedicated?" You know, this is going to sound blasphemous, but "If God called them here to serve, why do they need money? God will provide." And then we tell somebody, "Be fruitful, multiply, have children," but we don't want to give enough money to buy shoes for their children. I think this attitude has changed very much in recent

years, but when I launched into nonprofit work, I saw people that literally had to leave organizations because they could not get the health insurance that was adequate to take care of the most basic needs of their family. It might sound like a side issue in leadership, but where do you want to invest your resources? If you tell me that your team members are your most important asset, why do you treat them like that?

233. Laurie: *"Ladies and Gentlemen serving Ladies and Gentlemen" - Wouldn't that be really a nice way to be able to talk about organizations going forward?*

234. Alan: Well, you know, it's a heartbeat of mine. *The New Gold Standard* is one of the books that I always recommend people read.

235. When Ritz-Carlton sold to Marriott and when Simon Cooper became President, he wanted a book about the mystique - how they did it. He hired this author, and they de-Christianized it. Bill Johnson had Bible verses that backed all of his stuff, like the Fourteen Points, and everything. Everything in Johnson's mind had what you would call a biblical or a scriptural basis for what he did. "Ladies and Gentlemen serving Ladies and Gentlemen" came obviously from the biblical principle "due unto others." But the book, even with the verses taken out because it was written as a secular book, still is powerful, and it's one of the first ten books I recommend to everyone who leads a team. If you've ever been to a Ritz-Carlton or spent any time there, you will know what I mean.

236. In my case, how do you get people to leave home and leave their practice, especially in the case of small firms and single practitioners, when they don't even get vacation time? They don't get paid if they take hours off and they're not working. How do you get them to come to classes for a week and agree to give you four hundred and fifty pro bono hours over the next three years after they come to your class that they've sacrificially gone to?

237. Well, I found out one of the things was to take them to really, really nice places. So, we'd go to the Ritz-Carlton in Cancun. Now we'd go in July, when it's hotter than blazes. But it's a five-star resort. It's incredibly beautiful, but the hotel is half full. Bringing in a group

at a very much discounted rate is a whole lot better than having empty rooms. And so, it was a win-win-win.

238. One time I had a writer attack me. This was a secular writer, and they said, [paraphrasing] "This horrible ministry ADF is wasting money. It takes all these people to exotic vacations in the Ritz-Carlton." So, I called them up. I said, "I invite you to come. Sit in and see what the vacation looks like with the twelve-hour days that these people have. They do get a whole afternoon off, and they can bring their family. And then I'll ask you to tell me what you think would be a fair room rate for a nonprofit." They ended up not attacking us anymore. The facts cleared it up. So, you know, we just said, "We want to give people the best."

239. Laurie: *Right.*

240. Alan: And then people gave us the best. ADF now has had, I don't even know the number, but well over one hundred million dollars of pro bono time reported back to us. At one time those Academy sessions were running about eighteen to one ROI [Return on Investment] for ministry dollars. I mean definable, discernible, touchable dollars as opposed to just speculative.

241. Laurie: *I'm sure there's always that intangible benefit for the person doing the pro bono - providing a feeling that they've had meaning in their life.*

242. Alan: Yes, and one of the things we found was that after a person did an average of two cases pro bono, we have them for life because they would get such a reward out of it. There were two different individuals, one from Anchorage, Alaska, and one from Denver, Colorado, that we gave awards to when they crossed the two-thousand-hour mark of reported pro bono. Two thousand hours is the average number of hours a lawyer bills to work in a year in a law firm. So, these two individuals crossed the one-year volunteer service mark. You know, I wondered how they made a living!

243. Laurie: *They clearly must have felt it was worthwhile!*

244. Alan: That's the kind of thing that gives you great joy.

245. Laurie: *Well, those individuals had clearly become leaders in doing the work well that God had called them to do. What other factors have contributed to ADF's incredibly high win rate?*

246. Alan: How do you achieve success in court? Well, you work hard. I used to have a saying when I first got into this area of law: I said, "If they have a fish on their business card - run!" Now, what did I mean by that? Sadly, in my young experience as a lawyer, I encountered a number of people that put fishes on their business cards (not only lawyers, but in other professions as well) and I found that in some cases, certainly not all cases, but I found in some cases, people traded on their relationship with people as members of their faith group. Sort of exploiting, in some ways, that relationship rather than excelling in their legal or other work. I had a couple of really, really negative experiences with that in my business, in my early career. So I actually had a little talk. I said, "If somebody's trading based on their faith and they have a fish on their card to do so - run!" Because you have to really excel in this area. There are no excuses. You can't get by without doing the very, very best and digging in really hard. So that's one attribute: we train people well, and we work very, very hard. And we can't, of course, discount God's amazing grace and the power of prayer.

247. One of the challenges we realized from early on was: How do you get a case in front of the Supreme Court? There were a lot of bad cases, a lot of bad precedents that when we launched ADF we wanted to overcome. One of those most famous ones is *Roe V. Wade*, which I think everybody knows, even members of the Supreme Court all recognized, including the late Ruth Bader Ginsburg, it was not well founded in the Constitution. It was part of this (back to my law school experience) what we might call the living, breathing, flexible, rolling, whatever term you want to use Constitution. And so that was one that we pursued. There also were a number of other cases as far out in left field without a constitutional basis as *Roe V. Wade*.

248. So how do you get a case to the Supreme Court? The fastest way to get to the Supreme Court is by winning some cases and losing some others. That may sound very strange but there are a number of federal circuit courts in the United States. For example, Arizona is in the 9th Federal Circuit; Georgia is in the 11th Federal Circuit, and so forth. What we learned as we developed cases and we would bring

them to court in different circuits is that you would get different rulings, sometimes a completely opposite ruling. Now here's a little problem. We have one Constitution, but we might have two, three, four courts telling us what the Constitution means or how it's applied to a circumstance. It's called a split in the circuits. The only court that can resolve a split in circuits is the U.S. Supreme Court. So it's a strange thing to say that we had to lose to win in order to get some cases heard by the Supreme Court. Not that we wanted to lose any cases. You'd like to win everything on behalf of your client, but some of these were long, long treks.

249. You know the road to seeing the reverse of *Roe v. Wade* was fifty years long. I was involved in a case in Kentucky, just months after I was out of Law school. I wasn't a counsel of record, but I went into court to help a friend of mine who was defending a regulation enacted in the Commonwealth of Kentucky that had certain requirements for doctors. In those early days, before the later *Casey* case came down, the Federal District Court struck some of the most basic kinds of health and safety requirements relating to abortion that they would have never stricken in other areas of healthcare. Note, abortion is not healthcare, but that's what the courts call it, and that's what the abortion advocates call it, but it is not healthcare. So that [split in the circuits] was how we got to the point of having cases heard in the Supreme Court.

250. ADF has advanced forward; it now has in this term of the U.S. Supreme Court - this calendar year - we'll have three cases that have already been granted review: One was argued a few days ago [at time of interview], the South Carolina case, on defunding Planned Parenthood,[4] tomorrow the U.S. Supreme Court will hear a case involving a Charter School in Oklahoma,[5] and then this fall the court will hear a case involving a Christian counselor from Colorado, who has had her First Amendment, free speech rights, and her ability to counsel her clients restricted by a Colorado State law. Colorado has in essence decreed that counselors cannot help people who are unhappy with same sex attraction or gender issues unless it is to

---

[4] https://www.supremecourt.gov/opinions/24pdf/23-1275_e2pg.pdf

[5] https://www.supremecourt.gov/opinions/24pdf/24-394_9p6b.pdf

affirm them in those concerns. It's not to help them if they want to find their way out of those kinds of things. It's a very, very strange law that basically prohibits one side of speech and not the other. ADF represents a counselor from Colorado.

251. One of the more famous ADF series of cases involved Jack Phillips. Jack was an artist in Colorado who went into the bakery business, and he combined his artistic skills with baking; he made cakes that were literally masterpieces. The name of his organization was Masterpiece Cakes and that had a little double meaning because it was the Master of the universe, God, that he was serving, but the cakes were also a sort of masterpiece. People who saw his work were astounded at the detail, and he developed quite a reputation. But he had also, through the years, declined to do certain things. A horror movie being filmed in the area asked him to make some custom cakes, but he wouldn't do it. He declined to do Halloween. I didn't know there were divorce celebrations, but apparently there are, and he declined to do those.

252. Finally, a couple of people came in demanding that he make a cake to celebrate their same sex relationship, their so-called "marriage." He declined respectfully and told them he'd sell them any goods in the shop, but he would not make a custom cake, celebrating something that was contrary to his faith. Of course he was brought up on various charges. He was ordered to keep track of everything, and he had to shut down roughly half his business. He and his family members were ordered to undergo sensitivity training to overcome their biblical beliefs. Ultimately, he won that case at the U.S. Supreme Court, only to be subject to two more actions after the Supreme Court case; the second one was dismissed, and then a third one that finally was disposed of in the Colorado Supreme Court more than a decade after the beginning of the first one.

253. In the meantime, another case had come up under a similar law for a company called *303 Creative* where a woman who did website designs for weddings was also subject to the Colorado decree. She was not willing to make websites for anything other than God's plan for marriage between one man and one woman. That case was brought to the U.S. Supreme Court while Jack's third case was pending in the State Supreme Court. So these things get complicated. There was more than a decade of incredibly expensive difficult

battles, and many cases leading up to the U.S. Supreme Court granting review of Jack's original case with a lot of losses, a lot of pain, and a lot of suffering along the way. But finally, through perseverance and because God's people provided the funding and the ability, ADF was able to carry forward and win.

254. Laurie: *Right now, there is quite a bit of debate regarding the power of the courts relative to Executive Orders and Directives. Can you speak to this in view of the Constitutional Originalism?*

255. Alan: There are three branches of government, and each branch has clearly delineated powers under the Constitution. An executive order is something that has always been within the purview of the civil authority. They date back to George Washington, the first person to hold the Constitutional office. If you remember, we had the Articles of Confederation. There were a number of so-called Presidents before George Washington, but he was the first President of the Constitutional United States. I don't believe I'm incorrect to say that every President has executed executive orders. The question that the courts are hammering out is one that is actually both complex and simple. The simple thing is, if it's within the President's Constitutional power to order what he orders, it's clearly okay. If he exceeds the bounds of his authority, it's not. That is what these cases are hammering out. We've already seen in some cases that some of the lower courts have been reined in by the Supreme Court, but it's very hard without the specific facts of the case to make a statement other than what I've already said.

256. If people recall, under the administration of Barack Obama, he was also one to use the executive order for some pretty strong decrees. So even in the most recent times, it's not unusual to see a President using executive orders. I think what's got everybody's attention is so many so quickly, and then the argument over whether or not he [President Trump] had the power in some of these cases. But just, for example, President Trump has issued a decree to abolish the Department of Education at the federal level and return it to the state level, but I think the decree was limited to the extent that it was

permitted by law.[6] Again, I can't tell you about any specific [executive order or directive], but that's the overall arching principle.

257. Laurie: *What is Moot Court and Amicus Briefing for a non-lawyer?*

258. Alan: A Moot Court is basically a practice court for when you're going to go before a real court. Especially in the Appellate court, you're going to have anywhere from three to nine judges who are going to be peppering you with questions. I don't know if you've ever listened to any recording of the Supreme Court arguments, but in about thirty minutes, there might be fifty or sixty questions fired at a counsel. People often say, "How do you have time to say anything you want to say at all?" In some cases, they almost never do, except in answer to the questions. You don't want to go into that field without being ready. So, a Moot Court is actually prep time. It'd be like, if you think of an athletic event, practicing running down the field, catching the ball, doing whatever the sport might be. So, a Moot Court is actually like a dress rehearsal.

259. Amicus briefs are a friend of the court briefs, and what we do there is - okay, you're going to laugh - only lawyers call a fifty-page document a brief.

260. Laurie: *Yes, that did get a laugh!*

261. Alan: And then there are lots of footnotes usually, and lots of explanations, but seldom in a case at the High Court can you say all you want to say in fifty pages. It sounds funny to say, but there are many, many people who have different viewpoints. And so, for some of these Supreme Court cases, part of the work of ADF was to assemble a group of amicus, of friends, who would file briefs and support. For example, in some of these cases, a dozen or more State

---

[6] Sec. 2. Closing the Department of Education and Returning Authority to the States. (a) The Secretary of Education shall, to the maximum extent appropriate and permitted by law, take all necessary steps to facilitate the closure of the Department of Education and return authority over education to the States and local communities while ensuring the effective and uninterrupted delivery of services, programs, and benefits on which Americans rely. https://www.whitehouse.gov/presidential-actions/2025/03/improving-education-outcomes-by-empowering-parents-states-and-communities/

Attorneys General have filed supporting arguments on behalf of their state government.

262. You can also have various groups. The USCCB [the United States Conference of Catholic Bishops] appears in amicus briefs for the courts quite a number of times during the years stating what the views are of the Catholic Church and the bishops in the United States. You may have individual bishops who appear. You know Bishop Olmsted. When he was Bishop of the Diocese of Phoenix, I was involved in some litigation where there was a church bell case, and an evangelical pastor was actually prosecuted and sentenced to the possibility of jail time for ringing his church bells. They were supposed to be too loud or something, and legal action was brought on behalf of a parish in the Diocese of Phoenix and a number of other churches. There was a win at the U.S. District Court, because what we were able to show is that ice cream trucks had louder and more obnoxious bells than the churches and were exempt! The church rang its bell three or four times a day and the public school next door to one of the churches rang its bell twelve times a day and it was twice as loud as the church's bell. Yet the pastor was going to be prosecuted. Sometimes it's good to bring friends into court actions and win for the common good. And to my knowledge, there have not been any church bell prosecutions threatened in recent history.

263. **Laurie:** *That's good, really good! Alright, you probably feel like you're in that Moot Court right now with me firing these questions at you, but you have plenty of experience with that! You've been involved in many innovative projects like the Center for Academic Freedom, the Corporate Resource Council, the Christmas Project, and the public prayer effort. Can you talk about those innovative projects and how you got them started? I'm thinking of inspiration for the Tepeyac Leadership Initiative students and their commitment statement at the end of the program.*

264. **Alan:** On the Leadership Points Summary (See Appendix), it has this phrase, "Creating the capacity to respond to opportunity." One of my life beats, or whatever you want to call it, is that when you are building something, you want to create a capacity to respond to the opportunity that God puts before you, and you never know what that will be.

265. Now, one of the problems in a nonprofit, charitable faith world is that there are more opportunities than you have resources to meet. So you can't say yes to everything. When people came to me with ideas that would cost something, they would say, "Well, we'll fund the beginning of this idea." One of the things I'd say was, "How about funding it for three years, if you think it's such a great idea?" I never had anybody take me up on that. They wanted me to launch something and then figure out a way to fund it. So that's what we did. We said, "We're open." One of our other little adages is, "Good ideas come from anywhere and everywhere."

266. When we were running DC Ranch Country Club during Covid, the general manager and I basically made a little covenant that we were going to keep every team member on health insurance, no matter what it took. Then we enlarged it and said, "We want to keep everybody on the payroll, no matter what it takes," because, remember, everything was shut down. We didn't know where it was going to go. And this also applied to ADF. We said, "Give us your ideas."

267. So, one of the team members at the Country Club started making candle kits. We had another team member making and selling popsicles. We turned the place into a grocery store; we used the Tee Time sheet, you know, where you set your Tee Times, to have your grocery pickup time. We had all these supplies that we couldn't use because the restaurant was closed, and then it was very moderately open. So, we'd sell to people things they couldn't get in the store. People would go online, they'd fill in their order, and then they would have a time to come pick it up. We ended up keeping every single team member on, not only in health insurance, but on payroll. And at ADF, the same thing.

268. So these opportunities came along, like the Christmas project; people don't recall, but there was a real attack by the ACLU on the public celebration of Christmas. We began to take a series of cases and fight this. We began to have some success in the court standing up against these so-called establishment of religion things. Bill O'Reilly, who used to be a big name on Fox News, got interested in the project and we made numerous appearances on those programs. We developed a whole campaign. We had the capacity to respond to the opportunity. He partnered with us, and we had literally within a

one-year period, a ten percent change in the USA Today polling on the acceptability of saying "Merry Christmas." We went positive by ten points in a year with that campaign, among other things, as well as making legal progress. Now you rarely hear of an attack on Christmas. There's always some complaint, but legally there are not that many cases because we substantially cleared the field and most of that area of argument. And so, each of these things that came along - some were by design and some were brought to us - were worth grabbing, among the many, many things that weren't.

269. Laurie: *One of your leadership points that I don't think we've talked about too much is the no-debt policy. I imagine that it is important when you're serving on a board.*

270. Alan: Yes, at Alliance Defending Freedom, one of our founders who joined with us was a gentleman named Larry Burkett. He's been dead for quite a number of years. But Larry had an evangelical apostolate or ministry called Christian Financial Concepts. Larry really sought Scripture, and he tried to teach people sound principles; basically, how to live a good life and to stay out of trouble. He discovered in his research that one of the biggest obstacles to marital success is debt. You know, couples getting into a credit card mess, buying too big of a house - all those kinds of things. I'm sure that everybody who reads this would have their own stories to tell about debt problems.

271. He [Larry] particularly suggested that apostolate ministries should stay out of debt. They should only do those things that they have the funding to do. Our board adopted that as a policy; we only made an exception one time and that was to buy a building where we had half of the money in advance, and we had a pretty sure means of paying. Also, we took out a one-year mortgage for a small amount of money so that even if things had collapsed, we would have come out ahead.

272. We just found the no-debt policy to be prudent. As I counsel with and work with so many different apostolates, I have found that debt has been an albatross for quite a number of organizations, including some of our Religious Orders. They borrowed a lot of money to acquire a property beyond the means of their ability to

support it, or they borrowed money to rehabilitate crumbling infrastructure buildings, and so forth and then they can't keep up.

273. There are not a lot of people who want to really service debt. It's not a really appealing donor thing. "Dear donor, would you pay off my debt that I'm behind on?" They'd say, "What kind of organization are you running?" So, if you just stay within your means maybe you won't move as quickly, but you'll move more surely.

274. Laurie: *That sounds like good business advice. You mentioned The New Gold Standard [by Joseph A. Michelli] as one of the first ten books you would recommend professionals read. Do you have any others?*

275. Alan: If we are talking about the business side of running an organization, I always think of *Good to Great, Built to Last,* and *How the Mighty Fall* by Jim Collins. He is interesting. He allegedly left Stanford Graduate School of Business because he didn't write enough and then he out published all of the other faculty; they invited him back to teach some more. There are people who are a little confused because they think books get dated when they get to be ten or twenty years old.

276. Another one that I recommend is [W. Edward] Deming's *Out of the Crisis.* Deming was the expert who was brought over by MacArthur after World War II to rebuild Japan; He was a MIT Professor. Another is called Peter Drucker's *The Essential Drucker,* which was actually put together by some students of Peter Drucker. Basically, much of all modern management goes back to Drucker and to Deming. So look at Deming's Fourteen Points. Look at Drucker's "The purpose of a business is to create a customer." You create a customer through marketing and innovation. If your marketing is good enough, your sales will take care of themselves, etc., etc. These are very important things.

277. So if you're trying to build a Catholic apostolate, you need to market it. You need to be innovative. Look at what Steve Zabilski did with the St. Vincent de Paul Chapter in the Diocese of Phoenix. It's both innovative, every day there's something new being added, and it's marketed well.

278. Laurie: *What about your own books? You live and breathe leadership!*

279. Alan: Well, except for the Eisenhower book, everything I've written was for a particular moment in time when something needed to be addressed. The *ACLU vs America: [exposing the agenda to redefine moral values* /Alan Sears and Craig Osten], for example, was when we were launching into this response to the cases the ACLU had done. There was this mistaken view where people said, "Well, the ACLU used to be a good organization. It just kind of got off track." Well, no. Go back to Roger Baldwin, who was Margaret Sanger's counselor and supporter; you can, in many ways, say Planned Parenthood would not have become what it is without Roger Baldwin and the ACLU. So, we needed to clarify the history.

280. My favorite book I've ever been involved in is *The Soul of an American President. The Untold Story of Dwight D. Eisenhower's Faith.* You know I love history, so I read hundreds of history books. I really fell in love with World War II history because I saw incredible parallels to our current moment with how you could win battles. I began going to Normandy and then taking friends with me. Then it became a tour that I would lead periodically. I've been there quite a number of times. So, one of my annual lecture series became The Virtues. My Virtue of Perseverance lecture was about Dwight Eisenhower. I asked myself a really obvious question, what gave him his perseverance? If you read the epilogue of the book, it will explain the story: I went on a detective search to determine if he was just talking about religion, or if it was deep. The book gives you my answer.

281. Laurie: *Okay, I look forward to reading that! One of my favorites is Freedom's Forge by Arthur Herman. Have you read that one? It's a World War II history book, and it was required reading at the Eisenhower Institute for a workshop I went to there.*

282. Alan: That's great. Eisenhower was an amazing leader. Look at all he accomplished after he saved Europe in World War II, with NASA, the Saint Lawrence Seaway, and the interstate highway system. Also, the sadness of Little Rock [School Integration Issue], but the essential necessity of it. On and on it goes. So quite an amazing person.

283. Laurie: *What do you hope for this book?*

284. Alan: What I would really hope is that the book would give some blessing and guidance to young people who are interested in getting involved in public life who want to combine their faith and their life. One of the purposes of the Blackstone Fellowship is to help people understand that we are to integrate all aspects of life. One of the things that you're really taught [incorrectly] in professional graduate schools, like law school, is the segregation of the professional and the personal and how the two aren't to be overlapped.

285. In fact, I'll never forget; I won't say the name, but one of the former justices of the Arizona Supreme Court was at one of my continuing education classes. One of the question-and-answer sessions was going on and this justice interrupted. He said, "If you confuse morality with ethics, you may find yourself in great trouble as a lawyer." Then he kind of explained what he meant by that, and I wasn't very pleased with his explanation. He was essentially saying that morality was something that was made up by people of faith, whereas ethics were this fixed standard in law that you could judge activities by. It was just bizarre! It really stuck out. And this was also a judge who was noted for not being an originalist judge.

286. When you think about that line of reasoning and what so many people are subjected to in their education, it really is radical to a lot of people to think about the fact that you're supposed to be 24/7, 365 days, the same person in all things, in all ways. I can't imagine our team segregating their personal life and their professional life in terms of how they live that life and the values that they portray. So maybe that's a long way to say, I hope people can find guidance for a 24/7 Christian life.

287. Laurie: *Well, thank you for your courage, your perseverance, and for sharing what truth is.*

289. Alan: You're very kind to call it courage; it is probably more perseverance than courage. It's just you're there in the moment, and you just have to endure. I think that a lot of times when you look back on things people think, "Wow! That was really courageous to do." And you're just thinking, "I need to survive. I need to get through this, this month, this moment." And so, this is not like being brought into combat and shot, but there is some pretty rough combat. There are some pretty cruel words, and there are people threatening all the time. Anybody who's involved in high level public policy or litigation draws fire.

290. We often say the shots in front you can deal with; it's the shot from behind by your fellow believer that discourages you. That is one of the things with our Church and why I think Tepeyac Leadership Initiative is so important for formation because we need people to stand by our sides and to have our backs. That may be one of the great things that Cristofer and all of you accomplish: help people find other people to stand with them and help hold their arms. Remember how Aaron and Hur helped Moses raise his arms? [Exodus 17:12]

291. Laurie: *Yes!*

292. Alan: And again, you ask, "What can the laity do?" Well, okay. You hear that so and so have been admonished by their employer because they did something good, something right. But they got in trouble for it, and maybe they just need somebody to come down and hold their arm, to come out with them for a drink and a little conversation. I guess that's a long, winded way to say, I hope people can find out how to live with an integrated life.

293. Laurie: *We've talked about your lifelong search for truth, your heart for servant leadership and your love of family. As our final wrap-up question, how would you define a life well-lived, and the friendship that God has called us to?*

294. Alan: If at the end of the day, you have no regrets in your relationships with the people God has put in your life – even the ones we don't particularly like. We all have many, many people cross our paths. As you said, we have our family, our loved ones, our friends. I think we all want to hear that line in Scripture, "Well done, good and faithful, servant." [Mathew 25:23] So that is how I would summarize my thoughts as to how to define success.

APPENDIX I

Leadership Principles

Derived from Leadership principles that built Alliance Defending Freedom (ADF)
©2019/2025
Alan Sears, Founding President, CEO & General Counsel Alliance Defending
Freedom, ADF International, ADF Foundation & Kingdom Alliance Builders
(with thanks to Bobb Biehl, a lifelong friend, and many years of ADF Team input)

We've seen some of what has happened, that the Lord has granted some degree of mercy and favor upon the legal ministry, the Kingdom-focused ministry of ADF, and some substantial growth has occurred as noted. I am asked often "What is the secret of the growth and the success of ADF?"

VISION and VALUES

First, we must explain, we don't know how successful we have been. We do not know what we've done that is most consequential to the Kingdom because it is the Lord who with His scale weights and measures results and outcomes, not us mere mortals. But to the extent we've been blessed to have any success at ADF, these **KEY WORDS** would be among the reasons:

▪ **VISION:** Define a clear vision of mission/purpose which is simple to communicate: 1) *"Keep the door open for the Gospel" through strategy; training; and funding to advance advocacy and transform the legal system for Christ. 2) "Creating the capacity to respond to opportunity." - and, 3) "We are here to win V Occupy until He comes."* (para. 48, 264)

▪ **PEOPLE:** Servant leaders like Edwin Meese. (para. 16)

▪ **HUMILITY**: Over 100 Bible verses admonish and guide us to stay on our knees; *"If any man desire to be first, he shall be the last of all, and minister of all."* Mark 9:35 (para. 25)

▪ **SERVANTHOOD**: Who Jesus was; the King of the Universe who emptied Himself to become a slave. Philippians 2:7 (para. 203)

▪ **FRIENDSHIP**: What the Lord called us to. John 15:13, 15 (para. 293)

▪ **ALLIANCE BUILDING**: Establish mutual cooperation and dependencies. Example: funding for allies - grants to what the world would call "competitors." 1 Thessalonians 5:11 (para. 53)

- **EXCELLENCE:** *"Gold Standard"* Most words cannot define excellence, but we can see, feel, touch, smell it V Mediocrity. *"If lawyers business card had a fish on it, we said 'run.'"* (para. 231 V para. 246)

- **NO-DEBT POLICY:** Larry Burkett taught us to avoid this ministry trap. (para. 269)

- **OPPONENTS:** We don't have enemies, we have opponents, and we need to fight them with honor in a way that honors our Lord and builds the possibility of relationships. Ephesians 6:12 (para. 120)

- **MAKING STARS OF OTHERS:** It's not about us - sharing credit by design - Reagan Sacramento & DC desk plaque: *"There is no limit to what a [man] can do or where he can go if he doesn't mind who gets the credit."* *"…humbly regard others as more important than yourselves…"* 1 Philippians 2:3 (para. 24)

- **PERSEVERANCE:** Like Ike/Eisenhower, not surrendering, not stopping no matter how unpleasant. (para. 280, 287)

- **ALWAYS CONVEYING HOPE:** By His word the Heaven is made. Serve Lord of Creation, for the faithful the best day is always ahead. (para. 283, 292)

- **ALL, EVERYTHING ROOTED IN JOHN 15:5:** God's mercy and Grace - *"Without Him we can do nothing"* - *"If foundations be destroyed what can the righteous do."* Psalm 11:3-7. (para. 224)

- **TEAM:** Always Team, Never "Me." (para. 228)

- **EMPOWER THEM:** With Commander's Intent and get out of their way for innovation (good ideas from any/everywhere). Make it safe to, *"fail early, fail often, fail forward."* (para. 265)

- **LEARN:** Never punish for mistakes, only deliberate acts/coverups. (para. 170, 226)

"Grant me, O Lord my God, a mind to know you, a heart to seek you, wisdom to find you, conduct pleasing to you, faithful perseverance in waiting for you, and a hope of finally embracing you." (St. Thomas Aquinas)

"Show Me Your Friends and I'll Show You Your Future" (Unknown, see Proverbs 13:20)

APPENDIX II

Team Building and Development

Derived from Leadership principles that built Alliance Defending Freedom (ADF)
©2019/2025
Alan Sears, Founding President, CEO & General Counsel Alliance Defending Freedom, ADF International, ADF Foundation & Kingdom Alliance Builders
(with thanks to Bobb Biehl, a lifelong friend, and many years of ADF Team input)

BUILD AN All-GREEN TEAM - Our objective always

80% **Problem Solvers** - FIX the system/ eliminate roadblocks to our dreams.
15% **Goal Setters** - ADD to existing system/ start with end in mind.
5% **Opportunity Oriented** - ACCELERATE the game/ seize the unexpected.
*** Each sees the entire world differently

"The role of an organization is to maximize the strength of the individual and make the individual's weakness irrelevant." (Dr. Peter F. Drucker)

Thus, as a leader: *"How do we maximize this person's unique strength?"*

- Teach BOULDER CALENDARING - Teamwide and individually – get your world in order, protect yourself and them.

- Avoid BURNOUT - the *"Job-Demands-Resources model offers a simple equation: burnout = demands > resources."* - *"The simple cure for most burnout is to do less. Decrease demands. Take time off. Rest. Relax. Reset."* [7]

- Use TWO-DEEP - Identify and train your replacement by having them work alongside you.

- KEY DEVELOPMENT WORDS - Relationships, Results, Numbers (details/costs/projects), Dreams, Unique

- Use RED, YELLOW, GREEN for on-the-spot evaluations.

- Focus on RESULTS v ACTIVITY - *"Criticize/correct privately orally - praise publicly in writing"* (unless personnel/ HR files demand a record)

---

[7]   https://blog.candid.org/post/why-nonprofits-are-burned-out-and-ways-to-beat-burnout-today/

SEVEN DIRECT REPORT QUESTIONS:

Once your priorities (measurable problems, goals, opportunities) are clear, these reporting questions will keep you and your team focused on the boulders with NO SUPRISES and the objectives of GREAT TO GREATER:

* 1. What DECISIONS do you need from me?
* 2. What PROBLEMS/ RESOURCE issues are keeping you from your priorities?
** 3. What PLANS are you making (which haven't been discussed)?
** 4. What PROGRESS have you made? (Dashboard, numbers, charts, trends, etc.)
** 5. What is your single greatest unexpected SUCCESS since your last report? (or other time period TBD)
* 6. On a scale of 1-10, how are you PERSONALLY? Why?
* 7. How can I PRAY for you?

* 1:1/ Confidential items
** 1:1/ Team meeting items

All Team levels can use.
How often? Weekly, Bi-Weekly, or TBD.
No more than a single page!

So let it be said, *"If there is success to celebrate - it is a gift and blessing,"* and it will continue as long as we repel the arrogance of self-sufficiency, pride, stay on our knees and remember those Leadership Principles.

Thus, it's *"Saddle up & fight or sit back & surrender."* So, let's all saddle up!

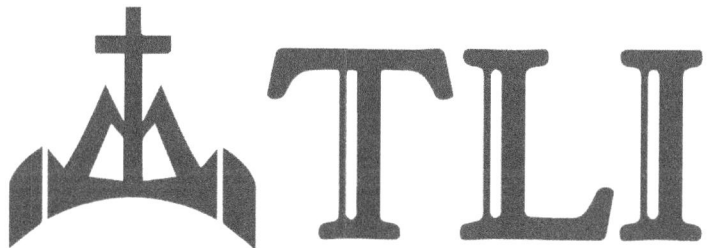

We hope you enjoyed this book.

Please consider supporting our efforts by learning about,
praying for, or financially supporting
Tepeyac Leadership, Inc.

Please visit:

TLIprogram.org
THLconference.org